Traveller's Wildlife Seychelles

Mike Hill
&
Dave Currie

Supported by Nature Seychelles

HarperCollins Publishers Ltd
77–85 Fulham Palace Road
Hammersmith
London W6 8JB

www.collins.co.uk

Collins is a registered trademark of
HarperCollins Publishers Ltd

First published in 2007

13 12 11 10 09 08

10 9 8 7 6 5 4 3 2

A catalogue record for this book is available from the British Library.

ISBN-10: 0 00 720149 4
ISBN-13: 978-0-00-720149-5

Editorial Director: Helen Brocklehurst
Editor: Emily Pitcher

Edited and designed by D & N Publishing, Hungerford, Berkshire.

Reproduction by Colourscan, Singapore.
Printed and bound in Hong Kong by Printing Express.

Contents

Foreword

Set in the western Indian Ocean 1,600km from the nearest continent, the Republic of Seychelles consists of more than 100 islands over a sea area larger than Peru (1,374,000km²). None of the individual islands is very large, but they all have complex and fascinating histories – some are weathered fragments of an ancient continent, others are the remains of ancient reefs that are now raised above sea level, and some are relatively recently exposed low islands of coral sand. The wildlife of the islands reflects this diversity, with mossy tropical forests on the upper slopes of the granite islands, and open, scrubby vegetation of widespread coastal shrubs on the lowest sandy islets.

People are a relatively recent addition to the islands, with humans first settling here in 1770. The earliest written accounts describe the accidental discovery of the central (granitic) Seychelles in 1609 by a ship of the British East India Company. Crewmembers described high islands, with abundant fresh water, coconuts, tame (easily caught) turtle doves, giant tortoises and tall forest trees. Apart from the ferocious saltwater crocodiles, the islands must have seemed a paradise, as they later did to General Gordon, who believed Praslin's Vallée de Mai to be the site of the Garden of Eden.

Time and human intervention have wrought changes over the intervening years; habitats have been altered for agricultural production, with plantations of coconuts coming to dominate the lowlands and cinnamon trees on the slopes. Some of the species unique to the islands have been lost through hunting and habitat change, while the introduction of pests, such as rats and cats, as well as invasive plant species, have all had a detrimental effect on the wildlife.

However, more recently the environment has changed again. Myself and a small group of other concerned citizens started the environmental movement in the early 1960s, and we joined with international scientists and organisations, such as the Royal Society and BirdLife International to increase knowledge of, and conserve Seychelles biodiversity. Thanks to the work of individuals, organisations and the Government of Seychelles, nature conservation has reversed the decline of endemic species, and visitors now have the chance to encounter indigenous birds and reptiles, some of which have only recently come back from the brink of extinction. Visitors and the income they generate now helps to support the continued conservation and restoration of the wildlife of these islands – wildlife that is described and illustrated in this book. I commend this book to you.

Kantilal Jivan Shah, Global 500 Laureate, United Nations Environment Programme; Medallist, Royal Society of Science and Letters, Norway; Lifetime Achievement Award, Rajiv Ghandi Foundation, India

The position of Seychelles.

Introduction

The Republic of Seychelles is a nation of about 150 islands stretching from Bird Island in the north to Farquhar in the south, about 900km distant, and from Coëtivy in the east to Aldabra in the west, a distance of over 1,100km. The islands that make up Seychelles differ greatly in their degree of isolation, geology, age, flora and fauna. The northernmost granitic islands are remote: 1,600km from mainland Africa, 1,050km from Madagascar and 2,500km from Sri Lanka. Although they were formed as part of a huge continent, their rocks have never been submerged in nearly 700 million years of existence. In the far southwest, and 1,150km from Port Victoria (Mahé), Aldabra is about 700km from Africa and 400km from Madagascar, the source of many of its species.

   In terms of their geology, history and wildlife, three broad groups of islands can be distinguished: the inner (or granitic) islands, the low coralline islands and the raised coralline islands.

The Island Groups

INNER (GRANITIC) ISLANDS   A group of about 40 islands clustered together on an undersea shelf of granite, the Seychelles Bank, which is now largely 45–65m below the sea surface. Most of these islands are themselves built of ancient continental granite at least 650 million years old, although two high islands, Silhouette and North, are made of more recent volcanic syenite rock, laid down during a period of volcanic activity about 60 million years ago. There are also two low coralline

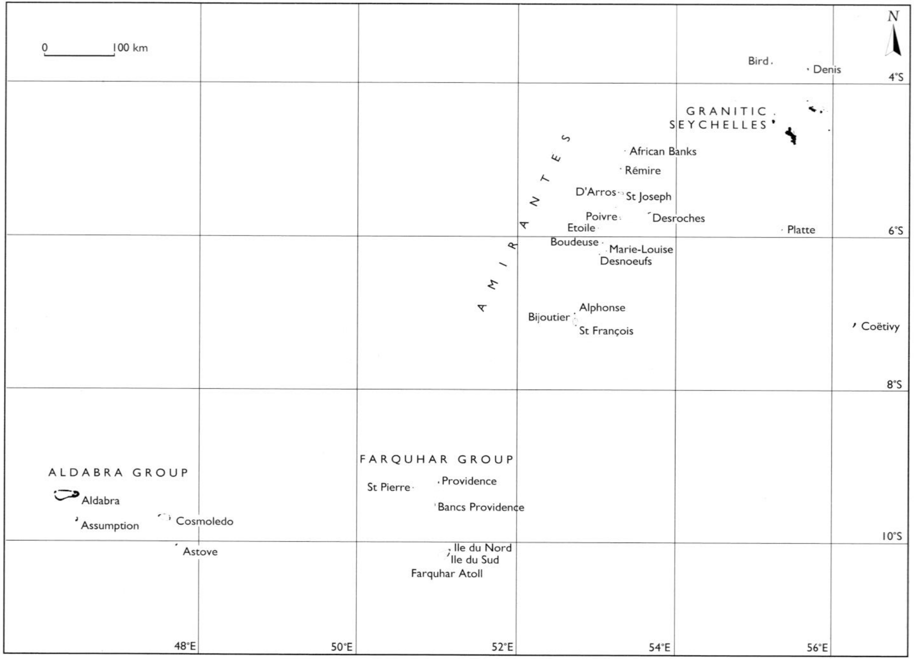
N
0
100 km
Bird
Denis
4°S
GRANITIC
SEYCHELLES
AMIRANTES
African Banks
Rémire
D'Arros
St Joseph
Poivre
Desroches
Etoile
Platte
6°S
Boudeuse
Marie-Louise
Desnoeufs
Alphonse
Bijoutier
St François
Coëtivy
8°S
ALDABRA GROUP
Aldabra
Assumption
Cosmoledo
Astove
FARQUHAR GROUP
St Pierre
Providence
Bancs Providence
10°S
Ile du Nord
Ile du Sud
Farquhar Atoll
48°E
50°E
52°E
54°E
56°E

The Seychelles.

islands of recent origin (Bird and Denis) on the shallow northern edge of the Seychelles Bank; their fauna and flora include some species typical of the granitics.

Once part of the southern supercontinent called Gondwanaland, the rock that now makes up the granitic Seychelles was wedged between that of Madagascar and India. As the continents drifted apart, Seychelles remained attached to India, drifting northward before becoming isolated about 65 million years ago. During periods of low sea level, such as the last ice age, most of the Seychelles Bank has been exposed as a single, large island, but even when global sea level was at its highest – several metres above current levels – most of the granitic islands remained above sea level, allowing the survival of unique endemic species.

The islands of the granitic Seychelles support the vast majority of the country's population (some 85,000 people) and have its only international airport (on Mahé). Most visitors do not venture beyond the granitics.

Low Coralline Islands The low coralline islands and sand cays were formed relatively recently from marine sediments – coral and shell sand, sometimes cemented by deposits of guano (seabird droppings). Almost all are less than 3m above sea level and have been inundated at times of increased sea level, last emerging around 5,000 years ago. The low coralline islands include the following groups:

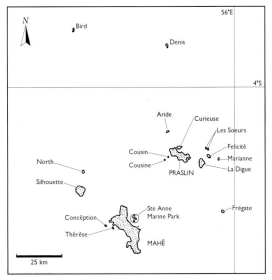

The inner Seychelles, including the granitic islands, Bird and Denis.

- Bird and Denis: two islands on the northern edge of the Seychelles Bank. The closest coralline islands to the granitics, and the most northerly islands of Seychelles.
- Coëtivy and Platte: two isolated coral islands 270km and 120km (respectively) south of Mahé.
- Amirantes: a string of 13 islands and atolls comprising about 26 islands in total, grouped on an undersea ridge, the Amirantes Bank. Three of these islands (the Alphonse group; Alphonse, Bijoutier and St François) are widely separated from the rest of the group, being at least 90km south of Desnoeufs.
- Farquhar group: two atolls made up of low islands (Providence and Farquhar Atolls) and one raised coralline island (St Pierre – *see* below) grouped on the Farquhar ridge, comprising 13 islands in total.

Compared to the granitic islands, the low coralline islands show little variety of habitats, and support a smaller number of species, many of which are widely distributed across the region. On most of the islands, terrestrial habitats have been substantially altered by human activity.

RAISED CORALLINE ISLANDS   The Aldabra group consists of three atolls – Aldabra, Cosmoledo and Astove – comprising about 66 islands, and Assumption Island. All of the Aldabra group and one island in the Farquhar group (St Pierre) are raised coralline islands. Like the more recent low coralline islands (*see* above), these islands have an oceanic origin, being formed first by reef-building corals perhaps 2.5 million years ago. The coral rock has been uplifted and now the highest rocks on Aldabra reach 8m above sea level (some of the sand dunes on Aldabra may reach 30m). The limestone surface is either flat (called 'platin') or eroded into many small sharp pinnacles ('champignon'). Together, the islands of Aldabra atoll have a land area of over 15,000ha – larger than Mahé, which would fit into the central shallow lagoon. In their history, the raised coral islands have been submerged and emerged above sea level several times, the most recent emergence being 125,000 years ago. Each time they were submerged, all terrestrial life on the islands was wiped out.

Today, Aldabra atoll itself is a World Heritage Site, inhabited only by a handful of wardens and scientists. Cosmoledo, Astove and St Pierre are now uninhabited.

Island Faunas and Floras

The granitic islands of Seychelles are relatively small – their combined land area is less than 1 per cent that of the largest of the Galapagos Islands – and remote, but very ancient. These factors mean that the flora and fauna of Seychelles are rather species-poor, when compared to other tropical sites, but relatively rich in species found nowhere else on earth – endemic species. Some of the endemics are descendants of species that were present here before Seychelles was isolated. Examples include the Coco de Mer and the endemic amphibians. Seychelles' amphibians are particularly unusual; amphibians are rarely found on continental islands as they cannot survive immersion in salt water. Other endemics are more recent colonists that crossed the saltwater barrier to reach the islands, adapting through evolution after colonisation to become new species.

The low coralline islands are of much more recent origin and have very few endemic species. However, the raised coral islands of the Aldabra group have been exposed for much longer and have developed a large endemic flora and fauna of their own; 22 per cent of their flora is endemic.

Island species often become especially large (island gigantism) or small (island dwarfism). A Seychelles' plant, the Coco de Mer, has the largest seeds and among the largest leaves of any plant; seeds can weigh up to 20kg each. Like several other island groups, Seychelles also has giant tortoises; adult Aldabran Giant Tortoises *Geochelone gigantea* regularly exceed 100kg and have been recorded up to 408kg in weight. On the other hand, one of the smallest frog species in the world is found on Seychelles: the tiny *Sooglossus gardineri*, *c*. 1.2cm long.

Another common feature of island ecology is called adaptive radiation. This occurs especially on remote oceanic island groups, where colonisation by new species is a rare event. These islands tend to be species-poor and, when a new organism arrives, it can evolve to fill many different ecological roles. The best-known example of adaptive radiation is that of 'Darwin's Finches' on the Galapagos, where a cluster of different species has evolved from a single ancestral finch species. The various finches fill different ecological niches, finding their food by different means, and evolved on different islands of the archipelago. There are relatively few examples of adaptive radiation in Seychelles; some exceptions are the endemic snail genus *Pachnodus*, the weevil *Cratopus* and the green geckos *Phelsuma*.

Flightlessness is another common characteristic of some island species. Island birds tend to lose the power of flight; because their island homes are usually free of predators, it is unnecessary, indeed positively dangerous, as they could be swept out to sea by storms. The Mascarenes once had several endemic flightless birds, including the Dodo and the

Red Rail on Mauritius, the dodo-like Solitaire and Rodrigues Rail on Rodrigues, and a flightless ibis on Réunion. Now the only flightless bird surviving in the western Indian Ocean region is the Aldabra Rail.

Notes on the Layout of this Book

This guide includes an introduction to the species and habitats of the Republic of Seychelles, including the granitic, low and raised coralline islands. It would be impossible to include all the species, especially for diverse groups such as the invertebrates and marine fish, but the aim is to show a selection of the prominent and important species you are likely to come across, including some of the interesting endemics and many of the plants and animals that have been introduced since humans first settled the islands and began to alter the ecosystems.

The guide takes a species-by-species approach, with most species being illustrated by a photograph of a typical specimen. Mammals, birds, reptiles, amphibians, fish and invertebrates (marine and terrestrial) are treated in separate sections. For plants, the treatment is slightly different, with species being grouped according to their principal habitat.

For all species covered, the information is presented as follows:

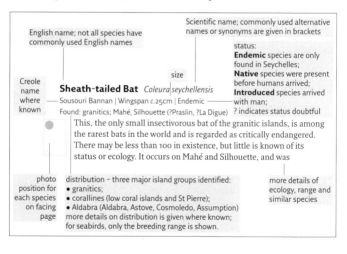

English name; not all species have commonly used English names

Scientific name; commonly used alternative names or synonyms are given in brackets

status:
Endemic species are only found in Seychelles;
Native species were present before humans arrived;
Introduced species arrived with man;
? indicates status doubtful

Creole name where known

size

Sheath-tailed Bat *Coleura seychellensis*
Sousouri Bannan | Wingspan *c.*25cm | Endemic
Found: granitics; Mahé, Silhouette (?Praslin, ?La Digue)

This, the only small insectivorous bat of the granitic islands, is among the rarest bats in the world and is regarded as critically endangered. There may be less than 100 in existence, but little is known of its status or ecology. It occurs on Mahé and Silhouette, and was

photo position for each species on facing page

distribution – three major island groups identified:
• granitics;
• corallines (low coral islands and St Pierre);
• Aldabra (Aldabra, Astove, Cosmoledo, Assumption)
more details on distribution is given where known;
for seabirds, only the breeding range is shown.

more details of ecology, range and similar species

For the plants, the following symbols indicate the growth habit of the species:

tree

herb

shrub

vine, climbing plant

OPPOSITE: Seychelles Scops Owl.

Mammals

Before human settlement, the granitic Seychelles supported just two species of land mammal, both bats; Aldabra had four bats and there were probably none on any of the low coralline islands. In contrast, the marine environment was quite rich in mammals, with dugong around some of the coralline islands and possibly also the granitics, several dolphin species, and large whales especially in deeper water around the edge of the Seychelles Bank and closer in to the coralline islands. There may even have been a species of seal, now long gone.

Following early exploitation and settlement by humans, this situation altered. Many land mammals were introduced, with feral populations of pigs, cattle, deer, goats, hares, rabbits, Tenrecs, cats, dogs and rodents becoming established. Marine mammals fared badly at the hands of man, with populations of some (seals, dugong) being lost and others being severely exploited. In the nineteenth century, a whaling industry targeted sperm whales to the north of the Seychelles Bank.

Today, the wild and feral mammal fauna of Seychelles is restricted to a handful of species of smaller terrestrial mammals, several bats, and a number of marine mammals, of which the most likely to be seen are the dolphins. In the granitic islands, the endemic insectivorous bat is now extremely rare, although populations of the Seychelles Fruit Bat seem relatively healthy. At least nine introduced mammal species still have permanent feral populations, but many of the larger introduced mammals have been exterminated on most inhabited islands, either deliberately or as a consequence of heavy hunting pressure in the late twentieth century. Where there were once feral populations of species such as pigs and cattle, these are now generally extinct. The most widespread introduced mammals of Seychelles are rats, which have occurred on most islands and may still be carried between islands accidentally. Rats have had a serious impact on native wildlife, threatening nesting seabirds, land birds and invertebrates. It is now possible to eradicate populations on smaller islands using poison bait, something that has been successfully achieved on several islands with a high conservation value.

OPPOSITE: Tenrec.

Native Land Mammals

Sheath-tailed Bat *Coleura seychellensis*
Sousouri Bannan | Wingspan *c.*25cm | Endemic
Found: granitics; Mahé, Silhouette (?Praslin, ?La Digue)

This, the only small insectivorous bat of the granitic islands, is among the rarest bats in the world and is regarded as critically endangered. There may be less than 100 in existence, but little is known of its status or ecology. It occurs on Mahé and Silhouette, and was previously known on Praslin and La Digue, where it may already be extinct. It roosts in granite caves by day and feeds in the evening and at night over marshes and damp forest at low altitudes.

Three insectivorous bats have been recorded in the Aldabra group, the widespread Mauritian Tomb Bat *Taphozous mauritianus* (Aldabra, Assumption; illustrated here), *Chaerephon pusilla* (endemic to Aldabra) and *Triaenops furculus* (Aldabra, Cosmoledo); the last two species are regarded as endangered (vulnerable).

Seychelles Fruit Bat *Pteropus seychellensis*
Sousouri | Wingspan 1.1m | Endemic
Found: granitics; most large and medium-sized islands | low corallines; occasional vagrant on Denis

Seychelles Fruit Bats are large (weighing up to 600g), with black wings and back contrasting with a bright orange-yellow head and neck. The subspecies *P. s. seychellensis* occurs in the granitic islands while *P. s. aldabraensis* is found on Aldabra and the other raised coral islands of the Aldabra group. The Aldabra form is slightly smaller, with whiter head and neck. During the day, they roost in groups in woodland treetops, emerging in the afternoon and evening to feed. They can fly between islands – for example crossing from Praslin to Cousin and other surrounding islands – to exploit seasonally available food sources. They feed on a range of native and introduced fruit trees and are involved in seed dispersal of native species including *Northea* and *Mimusops*. They also eat nectar and probably have a role in the pollination of trees such as *Sonneratia*. The animals are extremely noisy when at their feeding tree, and at large, popular feeding trees the noise of bats squabbling can continue for much of the night. The people of Seychelles traditionally exploit fruit bats as a food source, catching the animals in hooked nets strung between trees, but consumption has probably declined in recent years and the species appears abundant.

Tenrec   *Tenrec ecaudatus*

Tang | Length 26–39cm | Introduced
Found: granitics; Mahé, Praslin, Thérèse

The Tenrec is a small, hedgehog-like insectivorous mammal introduced from Madagascar via the Mascarene Islands, probably as a food item – Tenrecs are still eaten in Madagascar and Réunion, but not in Seychelles. It occurs from sea level to high altitudes on Mahé, Thérèse and Praslin, and is abundant in mid-altitude forests where it feeds on terrestrial invertebrates, lizards, and fallen fruit. In the dry season the animals aestivate underground. The young are tiny, only a few centimetres long, with pronounced pale stripes of spines. Adults lose the stripes, and are a uniform red-brown colour, with scattered spines in a coat of coarse hair.

Rats   *Rattus* spp.

Lera | Total length 35–42cm | Introduced
Found on almost all islands: granitics | corallines | Aldabra

Two species of rat are found in Seychelles. The Ship Rat or Black Rat *Rattus rattus* is a slim, relatively long-tailed dark rat with the ability to climb Coconut Palms and trees. It is found on most large or medium-sized islands and is an important predator of some endemic birds.

The Norway Rat or Brown Rat *Rattus norvegicus* is found on all the larger inhabited islands, especially around human habitation. It is usually brown with a cream belly, and is larger and bulkier than the Black Rat, with a relatively short tail. A less proficient climber than the Black Rat, it still has an impact on endemic birds and invertebrates.

Some islands have escaped the introduction of rats, and have a high conservation value; they include Aride, Cousin, Cousine, Récif, Bird, African Banks and St Joseph atoll. On Aldabra, some of the small islets are rat-free.

In addition to the two rats, House Mice *Mus domesticus* are present on many of the inner islands.

Black-naped Hare   *Lepus nigricollis*

Lyev | Length 50–60cm | Introduced
Found: granitics; Cousin

The Black-necked Hare is only found on Cousin where it was introduced directly from Mauritius in the 1920s or 1930s. It is a shy animal, most active in the early morning, evening and night.

The related rabbit *Oryctolagus cuniculus* is found on a few small islands where it can have a major effect on vegetation; e.g. Récif (granitics).

Cetaceans

WHALES AND DOLPHINS Our knowledge of the whale and dolphin fauna of the western Indian Ocean region is still far from complete, but dolphins are often seen around the islands of Seychelles. Species include the Spinner Dolphin *Stenella longirostris*, Spotted Dolphin *Stenella attenuata* and Bottlenose Dolphin *Tursiops truncatus* (or *T. aduncus*). The two *Stenella* species reach 2.2–2.3m long. In offshore waters, they can form huge groups of hundreds of individuals, but close to shore they are more likely to be seen in smaller groups. The Spinner can be recognised by its habit of leaping from the water and spinning on its longitudinal axis. The Spotted Dolphin's flanks are densely patterned with pale spots. The **Bottlenose Dolphin** (*a*) (*marswenn* in Creole) may reach 4m in length. It is dark grey-blue in colour, with a short, rather thick beak.

Larger whales are less frequent visitors, especially in the shallower waters around the granitic islands, although the deeper ocean to the north of Bird and Denis supported a whaling industry in the 19th century, when **Sperm Whales** (*b*) *Physeter macrocephalus* were hunted. This, the largest of the toothed whales, reaching 18m, still occurs around Seychelles. The Humpback Whale *Megaptera novaeangliae*, which may reach 15m in length, is mainly seen September–December off the edges of the Seychelles Bank. This whale has extremely long flippers and the tail flukes have a distinct central notch and knobbly trailing edge. It usually occurs in small groups and feeds on small fish and crustaceans.

A number of other species occur here, many only known from occasional strandings and rare sightings.

Sirenians – Dugong
The Order Sirenia contains only four species, all aquatic herbivores. Their nearest living relatives appear to be elephants, hyraxes and the Aardvark.

Dugong *Dugong dugon*
Vas marine | Length to 3m
Found: Aldabra; Aldabra

The Dugong or Sea Cow is a slow-moving marine mammal. Unlike the dolphins, Dugongs lack a dorsal fin. The nostrils are located at the tip of the broad muzzle, and males have small tusks in the upper jaw. They feed on seagrasses in shallow water, and are rarely seen in water over 75m deep. The Dugong probably once occurred around the granitic islands, but is now restricted to Aldabra. It is quite widespread in coastal waters of the Indo-Pacific, from East Africa to Australia, but nowhere is it particularly abundant.

Birds

The bird life of Seychelles is one of the great attractions of the archipelago to the naturalist, as it includes many endemic species or subspecies, and, in places, huge and spectacular concentrations of breeding seabirds. However, although very interesting, the resident fauna is rather species-poor. Because of the distance from mainland Africa, and the small size of the islands, rather few land birds occur here. So, while over 220 species of bird have been recorded in and around the islands, most of these are occasional vagrants. Only about 67 species now breed here. The granitic islands have just 28 breeding land bird species, 12 of which are endemic and nine introduced. Aldabra, a separate centre of endemism, has only 19 breeding land bird species. It has 11 endemic birds, most of which are regarded as races of species present elsewhere, usually Madagascar, and no introduced species. Nineteen species of seabird breed in Seychelles as a whole, but several of these are restricted to the coralline islands of the south – there are no breeding booby species in the granitic archipelago, for example. Twenty-five species of bird are regular non-breeding migrants, including 17 waders, seven seabirds and one duck (the Garganey). The waders and duck fly to Seychelles from the Northern Hemisphere to overwinter and are mainly present October–April, although first-year birds may stay all year round rather than migrating to their breeding grounds. Vagrant species are those that have been blown from their normal migration routes and so, like regular migrants, they are usually seen between October and April, especially after stormy weather and strong winds. Most vagrants stay for a short period before moving on or succumbing to exhaustion, but a few stay for prolonged periods.

In the 200 years since the islands were first settled by humans, several species have become extinct while the local range of other species has been severely restricted. Extinct endemics include the Seychelles Green Parakeet *Psittacula eupatria wardi*, Chestnut-flanked White-eye *Zosterops semiflava* (both from the granitic islands, exterminated in the 19th or early 20th century) and (probably) the Aldabra Warbler *Nesillas aldabranus* (the only warbler on Aldabra, last seen in 1983). Several of the surviving endemic species came perilously close to extinction, including the Seychelles Warbler (reduced to 26 on one island in 1968) and the Seychelles Magpie Robin (down to about 25 individuals on one island in 1970). Conservation actions have reduced these declines and barring catastrophe it seems unlikely that any more of the endemic birds will disappear. Recent years have seen efforts to eradicate introduced predators on many of the smaller islands in the granitic group, and these will provide further refugia for endemic bird species, several of which cannot survive alongside rats and cats.

The number of breeding birds in Seychelles has increased in recent years, with at least four species becoming established in the granitic islands in the last 25 years, including the Grey Heron, Black-crowned Night Heron, Ring-necked Parakeet and House Sparrow. The two herons probably colonised unaided – the Grey Heron had been a native breeder until being exterminated by hunting sometime before 1970. The others were deliberately released or ship-assisted. Today, the potential negative effects of introduced birds is recognised; several have become competitors or predators of native or endemic species, including the Barn Owl, deliberately introduced to control rats and now a pest itself on the seabird-rich islands. As a result, eradication efforts have been undertaken against some of the newer colonists; Indian House Crows, introduced in the 1970s, were successfully exterminated before they could reach pest status, and recent efforts to control House Sparrows may also be successful, although for both these species there is the danger of continued recolonisation from cargo ships.

Because of the limited number of species, identification of Seychelles' bird species should be fairly easy from the photographs shown: where there is a danger of confusion, similar species are named for comparison. Others may be vagrants; check in *Birds of Seychelles* (Skerrett, Bullock and Disley, 2001).

Seychelles Magpie Robin.

Seabirds

SHEARWATERS: GENUS *PUFFINUS* Shearwaters are agile fliers, often seen flying low over the waves when fishing. They nest in burrows on predator-free islands. Colonies are busy at night when the birds make weird calls. The chicks were commonly taken as food in the past and salted (as 'fouke'). Poaching has severely affected populations on unprotected islands.

Wedge-tailed Shearwater *Puffinus pacificus*
Fouke | Wingspan 64–74cm
Breeds: granitics; predator-free islands including Aride, Cousin, Cousine, Récif, Mamelles | corallines; Bird, Amirantes (St Joseph, Desnoeufs, Marie-Louise)

A large, all-dark seabird with wedge-shaped tail. Birds are mainly at the burrow from August–February. Adults leave the colony before dawn and return at night, when they make ghostly wailing and warbling calls. Feeds on fish, crustaceans and squid caught underwater.

Audubon's Shearwater *Puffinus lherminieri*
Riga | Wingspan 64–74cm
Breeds: granitics; predator-free islands including Aride, Cousin, Cousine, Récif | corallines; Amirantes (St Joseph, Desnoeufs) | Aldabra; Aldabra lagoon islets

A smaller, white-bellied shearwater with rounder wings than the Wedge-tailed. The underwing is white with dark outer edges. Like the Wedge-tailed, this species nests in burrows on rat- and cat-free islands.

TROPICBIRDS: GENUS *PHAETHON* Large, white seabirds with long tail streamers; two species breed in Seychelles.

White-tailed Tropicbird *Phaethon lepturus*
Payanke | Wingspan 90–95cm
Breeds: granitics; almost all islands | corallines; Bird, Denis, Amirantes (D'Arros, perhaps other islands) | Aldabra; Aldabra (mainly lagoon islets)

A widespread large white seabird with black mask and wing bars, and long white tail streamers. A solitary breeder that nests all year round. On Cousin and Aride, the nests are scrapes on the ground. On islands with predators, the birds nest in trees, or on ledges of inland cliffs.

Red-tailed Tropicbird *Phaethon rubricauda*
Payanke Lake Rouz | Wingspan 104–119cm
Breeds: granitics; Aride only (a few pairs) | Aldabra; Aldabra (lagoon islets), Cosmoledo

Larger than the White-tailed, with a pure white body, red bill and a narrow red tail, often invisible in flight. A very rare breeding species in the granitic Seychelles – a few pairs nest on Aride. It is more common on Aldabra, and islands further south in the Indian Ocean.

Boobies: genus *Sula* Boobies are large, gannet-like seabirds. Four species once occurred in the Seychelles' archipelago. All have seen a huge reduction in breeding colonies since the settlement of the islands, with one species (Abbot's Booby) becoming locally extinct – now it breeds only on Christmas Island in the Pacific. Today, no boobies breed in the granitic islands, where they are only occasional vagrants. Colonies still survive in the coralline islands of the south, particularly the Aldabra group.

Masked Booby   *Sula dactylatra*
Fou Zenero | Wingspan 142–152cm
Breeds: corallines; Amirantes (Boudeuse, Desnoeufs) | Aldabra; Cosmoledo

A large seabird with black tail and flight feathers, black face mask (base of bill), yellow bill and white body and wings. The juvenile has a dark brown head and back, white breast and belly, and dark feet. Most Seychelles' colonies have been completely lost and only occasional singletons are seen around the granitic group. Breeds October–May; simple nests are built on the ground.

Red-footed Booby   *Sula sula*
Fou Bet | Wingspan 91–101cm
Breeds: corallines; Farquhar group | Aldabra; Aldabra, Cosmoledo

A large seabird with a white tail, distinct red feet, and a pale patch of bare skin close to the bill. The juvenile is brown, with a lilac bill and pale pink feet. This species has an extended breeding season, with birds at the nest for much of the year, and is the only tree-nesting booby in Seychelles, often nesting in mangroves. Colonies in the Amirantes and granitic group have been lost through predation and poaching, and only occasional vagrants occur there.

Brown Booby   *Sula leucogaster*
Fou Kapisen | Wingspan 132–150cm
Breeds: Aldabra; only on Cosmoledo

A large, mainly brown seabird with a white belly, yellow bill and yellow feet. It nests on the ground in small colonies from March–December. This is now the rarest booby species in Seychelles.

FRIGATEBIRDS: GENUS *FREGATA* Frigatebirds are huge seabirds with a distinctive pterodactyl-like silhouette in flight. Two species breed in Seychelles (only in the Aldabra group) and both are epic long-distance fliers, being seen throughout Seychelles. The plumage of frigatebirds lacks water-proofing oils and their feet are not webbed; their huge wings quickly become waterlogged in the sea, so the birds cannot dive to fish. Instead, they catch their prey from the surface of the water – flying fish are an impor-tant food. In addition, they rob other seabirds, chasing adults returning to nesting colonies or roost sites until they drop or disgorge their catch. Away from the nesting sites, large roosts of hundreds or thousands of individuals may form in Casuarinas or other trees. In the breeding season, male frigate-birds display using an inflated scarlet throat pouch. Both species nest in trees, usually mangroves or *Pemphis*, when they are vulnerable to distur-bance by visitors. Young birds of both Seychelles' species have white or buff-coloured heads.

Great Frigatebird   *Fregata minor*
Gran Fregat | Wingspan 205–230cm
Breeds: Aldabra; Aldabra, Cosmoledo

The larger of the two native species, although it is often difficult to judge size in these birds. Males *(a)* differ from females *(b)* and juveniles *(c)* in having all-black plumage and also have a bright red throat pouch that they inflate in display when courting females. Display normally takes place at the breeding colonies, but males with partially inflated throat sacs can occasionally be seen around the granitic islands. The female has a white breast and throat, the white not usually extending onto the underside of the wings. The juvenile is similar to the female, with a white head. Breeding activity takes place for much of the year, as the chick takes up to six months from hatching to fledging, relying on its parents for food for a year after fledging. Pairs cannot breed every year. Twig nests are built in the tops of mangroves, and a single egg laid, usually between August–January.

Lesser Frigatebird   *Fregata ariel*
Pti Fregat | Wingspan 175–195cm
Breeds: Aldabra; Aldabra

Both male and female Lesser Frigatebirds have narrow spurs of white on the underside of each wing; females also have a large white patch on the breast. Like the Great Frigatebird, the male has an inflatable throat pouch used in sexual display. The breeding sites differ slightly from those of Great Frigatebirds; nests are built lower in trees or shrubs, and the single young is dependent on the adults for a shorter period. The main breeding period is June–October.

Terns: Family Laridae, Genera *Anous*, *Gygis*, *Hydroprogne*, *Sterna* and *Thalasseus* Terns are small-medium, rather slender seabirds, usually with a forked tail. They feed by diving for small fish and squid, or picking them from the water surface.

Brown, or Common, Noddy *Anous stolidus*

Makwa | Wingspan 77–85cm

Breeds: granitics; all predator-free islands, including rocks virtually devoid of vegetation | corallines; Bird and Denis, Amirantes (most or all islands), Farquhar group | Aldabra; Aldabra, Cosmoledo

An all-dark tern with a grey cap. Gregarious when feeding, but during the breeding season the bird is less social. Pairs nest in the top of Coconut Palms – where they may build a nest out of seagrasses or seaweed – or, on predator-free islands, on bare rocks (where no nest is made), e.g. L'Îlot Frégate, a small island off Frégate. The main breeding season is March–October (granitics and northern coralline islands) or September–March (Aldabra group).

Lesser Noddy *Anous tenuirostris*

Kelek | Wingspan 60–70cm

Breeds: granitics; Aride, Cousin, Cousine, Frégate | corallines; Bird, Denis, Amirantes (Rémire, Marie-Louise)

A smaller, slimmer noddy, with a much longer, narrower bill. Lesser Noddies nest communally in broadleaved trees, especially *Pisonia*, building simple, small platform nests of wilted leaves on the twigs and branches. A single egg is laid. Breeding occurs May–September on the granitic islands and on some of the Amirantes. On Aldabra, Lesser Noddies occur occasionally as vagrants.

Fairy, or White, Tern *Gygis alba*

Golan | Wingspan 70–87cm

Breeds: granitics; all vegetated islands | corallines; Bird, Denis, Amirantes (Alphonse), Farquhar group | Aldabra; Aldabra, Assumption, Cosmoledo, Astove

A pure-white tern found throughout Seychelles and often seen flying in pairs. There is no distinct breeding season and chicks can be found all year round. The Fairy Tern breeds in shrubs and trees, making no nest but laying a single egg directly onto the branch. The small grey chick has relatively large, clawed feet to hold onto its branch. This bird is one of the few seabirds that can breed successfully on islands infested with alien predators, and pairs can even be seen in trees in central Victoria, Mahé. However, breeding success is undoubtedly greater on islands free of predators such as Barn Owls and rats.

Caspian Tern *Hydroprogne caspia*
Dyanman Zean | Wingspan 130–145cm
Breeds: Aldabra; Aldabra

 A very large tern, with grey upperparts, white underparts, black legs and a shallowly forked white tail. The red bill is large and heavy, and the head has an extensive black cap almost developed into a small crest. Outside the breeding season, this black cap may be streaked with white. Worldwide, this tern has a very wide distribution, breeding in North America, Europe, central and north Asia and Australasia. Breeding sites are often inland beside lakes; Aldabra is its only oceanic breeding site.

Bridled Tern *Sterna anaethetus*
Fansen | Wingspan 77–81cm
Breeds: granitics; most of the 'seabird islands' including small rocks – Aride, Booby, Cousin, Cousine, L'Îlot Frégate, Mamelles, Récif, Sèche, Zave | corallines; Bird, Amirantes (Desnoeufs) | Aldabra; Cosmoledo

 A medium-sized tern similar to the Sooty Tern but differing in several ways. The Bridled Tern is slightly smaller, with grey rather than black upperparts, and lacks the white streak behind the eye shown by the Sooty Tern. A ground-nesting species, laying its egg on shaded rocks or among tussocky vegetation. Unusually among seabirds, it breeds on an eight-month cycle; within a colony, all birds breed around the same time, but breeding cycles of different colonies are asynchronous. The Bridled Tern breeds mainly on the northern islands of Seychelles, particularly the granitics; although birds are often seen on the coralline islands further to the south, few breeding colonies are known there.

Roseate Tern *Sterna dougallii*
Dyanman Roz | Wingspan 72–80cm
Breeds: granitics; Aride | corallines; Amirantes (African Banks, Etoile)

 A medium-sized tern with white underparts and grey upperparts, a long, deeply forked white tail and red legs. In the breeding season, the white parts of the plumage may be flushed rosy pink, and the bird has an extensive black cap and red bill. Outside the breeding season, black on the head is restricted to the nape, and the bill is black. A globally distributed bird, but of conservation concern as populations everywhere are declining. In Seychelles, few breeding sites are currently known – many have been lost through poaching. Some as yet undiscovered colonies may exist on the coralline islands.

Sooty Tern   *Sterna fuscata*

Golet | Wingspan 82–94cm

Breeds: granitics; Aride, Booby, Récif, L'îlot Frégate | corallines; Bird, Amirantes (African Banks, Desnoeufs, Etoile), Farquhar (Île Goelettes) | Aldabra; Cosmoledo

A widespread tern of tropical seas, and the only tern in Seychelles that is black above and white below. This colonial ground-nesting species breeds throughout Seychelles, on predator-free islands. Breeding occurs May–September, with each pair raising a single chick. Probably the most abundant bird in Seychelles, although many former colonies have been lost through habitat change and predation. The eggs of Sooty Terns are valued as a traditional food, and they were once gathered in huge quantities for export. Today, egg collection is regulated by the Seychelles' government and eggs from Desnoeufs, the only site regularly collected, are subject to an environment tax. The large, impressive colony at Bird Island is easily accessible and a 'must-see' if visiting the islands in the breeding season. The other large colonies are on Cosmoledo, Desnoeufs and Île Goelettes in the Farquhar group.

Black-naped Tern   *Sterna sumatrana*

Dyanman Likou Nwanr | Wingspan 61cm

Breeds: corallines; Amirantes (African Banks, St Joseph), Farquhar (Farquhar, Île Goelettes, Bancs Providence) | Aldabra; Aldabra, Cosmoledo

A small, white tern with a black stripe from eye to eye around the back of the head. Usually seen singly or in pairs around the lagoon or fringing reef of coral atolls. Nests on the ground on small, predator-free islands.

Greater Crested Tern   *Thalasseus bergii*

Dyanman Sardin | Wingspan 125–130cm

Breeds: corallines; Amirantes (Etoile), ?Farquhar (?Farquhar, ?Providence) | Aldabra; Aldabra, Cosmoledo

A large tern, with a rather shaggy black crest and a heavy yellow-green bill. Outside the breeding season, the extent of black on the head is reduced. This species is seen all year round at Bird, Denis and the granitic islands, and the northern Amirantes. Here it occurs singly or in small groups, fishing in shallow seas, resting on sandbanks, and patrolling shores in flight. However, it is not known to breed north of the southernmost Amirantes. The related Lesser Crested Tern *Thalasseus benghalensis* is smaller with an orange bill. It does not breed in Seychelles but occurs here annually.

Herons and Wading Birds

Grey Heron *Ardea cinerea*
Floranten | Wingspan 175–195cm | Native, Resident
Breeds: granitics; Mahé, Houdoul (yacht basin) | corallines; Amirantes, Farquhar group | Aldabra; Aldabra, ?Astove, Cosmoledo

The largest resident heron of the Seychelles, with grey plumage and black cap. The Grey Heron breeds on the granitic islands, Amirantes, Aldabra and may occur anywhere in Seychelles. In the granitic islands it is a relatively recent re-colonist; it was made extinct around 1970 by hunting, but returned as a breeding bird around 20 years later. It usually nests colonially and there are few breeding sites in the granitic group. The birds can be seen in freshwater wetlands including polluted streams running through Victoria, beaches, mudflats and mangroves. It is still more common further south in the Amirantes and the Aldabra group, where it fishes in lagoon waters, mangroves and shallow sea.

Cattle Egret *Bubulcus ibis*
Madanm Paton | Wingspan 88–96cm | Native, Resident
Breeds: granitics; Mahé, Praslin, Cousin, resident on many other islands | corallines; Amirantes, Farquhar group | Aldabra; Aldabra, Assumption, Astove, Cosmoledo

A small white heron with yellow bill and yellow-black legs. Breeding birds have patches of buff-yellow plumage on head, breast and back, a bright pink and yellow bill, and pink legs. This species has a near-worldwide distribution, having expanded its global range greatly in the 20th century. In Seychelles, it is native and abundant on the granitic islands, where it associates closely with man, feeding on flies at rubbish dumps and around Victoria's fish market, and catching insects on fields and sports grounds. It also occurs on some of the coralline islands, where it is an adaptable predator; on Bird and Desnoeufs islands it takes Sooty Tern eggs and young birds from the edge of breeding colonies. It breeds colonially in trees at several locations in the granitic islands and Aldabra.

Dimorphic Egret *Egretta dimorpha*
Zegret Blan e Nwanr | Wingspan 86–104cm | Native, Resident
Breeds: Aldabra; Aldabra, Astove, Cosmoledo

A medium-sized egret that occurs in two colour phases; the more common one is pure white with yellow lore and black bill, black legs and yellow feet. The rarer dark phase is dark grey with a white throat. Both phases can be seen around islands in the Aldabra group, where they feed in lagoons and mangroves. Nests colonially in low shrubs, with peak laying around November.

Green-backed Heron *Butorides striatus*

Manik | Wingspan 52–60cm | Native, Resident

Breeds: granitics; throughout | corallines; throughout | Aldabra; throughout

A very widespread species, found throughout the tropics and subtropics. In Seychelles, this tiny heron is found on almost all islands. It feeds in coastal shallows and mangroves, often fishing from a perch on rocks or logs, and catching small fish and other foods including small skinks, frogs, insects and crabs. It usually builds a solitary stick-nest in trees or shrubs. Two endemic races occur, one in the coralline islands (Amirantes and Aldabra) and one in the central Seychelles (pictured). It has a loud call, a sharp croak given when the bird is disturbed.

Black-crowned Night Heron *Nycticorax nycticorax*

Manik Lannwit | Wingspan 105–112cm | Native, Resident

Breeds: granitics; Mahé, Silhouette, Cousin | corallines; Amirantes (St Joseph)

This widespread heron is a recent natural colonist of the granitic and coralline Seychelles, first recorded breeding here in 1995. It is a stocky bird with distinctive plumage, often active in the evening and at night, when it feeds in shallow streams, mangroves or the sea. It breeds colonially at the top of trees, the adults flying out to feed at dusk making a duck-like quacking.

Yellow Bittern *Ixobrychus sinensis*

Makak Zonn | Wingspan 42–47cm | Native, Resident

Breeds: granitics; Mahé, Praslin, La Digue

A small yellowish heron, widespread in Asia and found on some of the larger granitic islands. A shy bird, best observed at quiet freshwater pools where it fishes in the shallows or from floating objects. Adults have orange-brown neck and beige-buff upper parts, while the plumage of juveniles (as pictured) is striped and mottled. Probably never common in Seychelles, it is increasingly threatened as freshwater marshland is lost to development.

Madagascar Pond-heron *Ardeola idae*

Gas Malgas | Wingspan 84–92cm | Native, Resident

Breeds: Aldabra; Aldabra

A small heron, restricted in Seychelles to Aldabra, where it is rare. Outside the breeding season it can be recognised by its white wings (obvious in flight) and brown back. The neck and head are streaky yellow-brown. In the breeding season, the birds have fine all-white plumage, pink legs and bright blue bill. Although not endemic to Aldabra, this species is regarded as 'near-threatened' globally. It is a colonial breeder, sometimes nesting alongside Dimorphic Egrets in eastern Aldabra. A rare vagrant in the granitic Seychelles.

Greater Flamingo *Phoenicopterus ruber*
Flaman Roz | Wingspan 140–165cm | Native, Resident
Breeds: Aldabra; Aldabra

An unmistakeable pale pink bird, with black primaries visible in flight. In Seychelles, the Greater Flamingo is only resident at Aldabra; this is one of only two breeding populations on oceanic islands worldwide (the other is on the Galapagos). On the low coralline islands and granitics, it may occasionally occur as a vagrant. Flamingos feed on small crustaceans, filtering them from the waters of shallow lagoons using the specially adapted bill. The nests are flat-topped conical mud structures, which have only been found occasionally at the eastern end of the Aldabra lagoon.

Madagascar Sacred Ibis *Threskiornis aethiopicus bernieri*
Ibis Malgas | Wingspan 112–124cm | Endemic Subspecies, Resident
Breeds: Aldabra; Aldabra

A large bird with white plumage, black featherless head and neck, long down-curved black bill and blue eye. Although regarded as a subspecies of a Madagascan endemic bird, this may be sufficiently distinct to be considered an Aldabran endemic species. It favours inland pools, where it feeds on crabs, snails and small vertebrates, and nests in shrubs close to the water. A rather rare bird, with up to 250 pairs breeding on Grande Terre, Aldabra (the only breeding site).

Moorhen *Gallinula chloropus*
Pouldo | Wingspan 50–55cm | Native Resident
Breeds: granitics; most large and medium-sized islands | corallines; Denis

A common wetland bird with a near-worldwide distribution. Native in Seychelles, where it occurs on and around freshwater and brackish marshes on many of the granitic islands and Denis. It breeds most successfully on the predator-free seabird islands, where it occurs in all woodland habitats. Elsewhere, it is more likely to be heard than seen; a short explosive call is given from cover.

Crab Plover *Dromas ardeola*
Kavalye | Wingspan 75–78cm | Migrant

A distinctive black and white wading bird with a huge, heavy black bill for catching and crushing crabs and other invertebrates. In Seychelles, it is a non-breeding migrant, present October–April. It is often seen in large flocks, especially on the coralline islands, where it feeds in shallow lagoons and on coastal mudflats. On the granitic islands, it usually occurs in smaller numbers. The Crab Plover breeds by the Red Sea and Persian Gulf. Unusually for a wader, it nests in burrows.

Sandplovers *Charadrius* spp.
Plovye | Wingspan 45–70cm | Migrant

Two species of sandplover occur as non-breeding migrants in Seychelles, and they are difficult to distinguish when not in breeding plumage. The Lesser Sandplover *Charadrius mongolus* (pictured) is smaller than the Greater Sandplover *C. leschenaultii*; the Lesser is about the size of a Common Ringed Plover, and has a more upright stance than the Greater. The Greater has longer legs and a more horizontal stance. Both species may be seen in mixed flocks with other small waders. They occur throughout Seychelles in September–April and feed on invertebrates on mudflats and sandbanks.

Common Ringed Plover *Charadrius hiaticula*
Plovye Kolye Nwanr | Wingspan 48–57cm | Migrant

A small wader, usually seen alone or in small numbers with other wading birds. It has orange legs and, in flight, an obvious white wingbar all along the wing. The bill may be dark, or orange with a black tip. In Seychelles, this annual migrant can be seen October–March. The similar but smaller Little Ringed Plover *Charadrius dubius* is an occasional vagrant in Seychelles; it has dark legs and lacks a wingbar.

Pacific Golden Plover *Pluvialis fulva*
Plovye Dore | Wingspan 60–68cm | Migrant

This fairly large plover occurs in small numbers each year in October–April. It can be seen feeding in shallow water and mudflats, and in open grassy areas. It can be distinguished from the related Grey Plover (*see* p.42) by its slightly smaller size and slimmer build, browner colour and lack of black 'armpits'. In breeding plumage (rarely seen in Seychelles), it has black breast, throat and face, edged with white.

Grey Plover   *Pluvialis squatarola*
Plovye Sann | Wingspan 71–83cm | Migrant

The commonest large plover of the Seychelles, occurring throughout the archipelago. It is usually seen singly or in small numbers on beaches and in coastal shallows, and in open grassy areas. In flight, it can be recognised by its distinctive black 'armpits'. Numbers are greatest September–April but some birds stay all year round. In breeding plumage (rarely seen in Seychelles), the Grey Plover has black breast, throat and face, edged with white.

Bar-tailed Godwit   *Limosa lapponica*
Limoza Lake Are | Wingspan 70–80cm | Migrant

An annual migrant seen throughout the Seychelles October–March. This large, grey-brown or red-brown wader has a long, straight bill. It feeds on invertebrates caught on coastal mudflats and sandbanks.

Common Greenshank   *Tringa nebularia*
Sifler Lapat Ver | Wingspan 70cm | Migrant

An annual migrant with pale grey, scaly upperparts, white underparts, greenish-grey legs and a long bill, slightly upturned towards the tip. Occurs singly or in small groups throughout Seychelles in October–March. This bird can be recognised by its feeding behaviour; it wades rapidly through shallow pools moving its head quickly from side to side, to catch small crustaceans and fish.

Whimbrel   *Numenius phaeopus*
Korbizo | Wingspan 80–92cm | Migrant

An abundant large wader with a long, down-turned bill, seen throughout the Seychelles, especially in October–March. Smaller than the Curlew, and has distinct dark brown stripes on the crown (Curlew has a mid-brown, mottled crown). It uses its long bill to probe for mud-dwelling invertebrates but may also catch crabs and other animals on the surface of the mud. Large flocks of 30 or more birds may form on the coralline islands.

Curlew   *Numenius arquata*
Gran Korbizo | Wingspan 80–100cm | Migrant

An annual migrant, mainly occurring October–March in smaller numbers than the Whimbrel. The Curlew is larger, with a longer bill than the Whimbrel, and the bill is dark with a pinkish base. Seen singly or sometimes in small groups throughout Seychelles.

Terek Sandpiper *Xenus cinereus*
Sifler Trakase | Wingspan 58cm | Migrant

A small, stocky wader with a long upturned bill that is yellow at the base, grading to brown at the tip, and bright yellow-orange legs. An annual migrant in small numbers, seen throughout Seychelles, but especially the northern islands in October–April. Often seen as a single individual in mixed flocks of other small waders.

Common Sandpiper *Actitis hypoleucos*
Sifler Bat Lake | Wingspan 40cm | Migrant

An annual migrant throughout Seychelles, mainly present October–March. A small, usually solitary, brown, short-legged wader seen along the margins of freshwater bodies and the sea. Distinguished from other small waders by its colour, short legs and bobbing motion.

Ruddy Turnstone *Arenaria interpres*
Bezros | Wingspan 50–57cm | Migrant

One of the commonest waders in Seychelles. A small, dumpy, rather short-legged bird. In breeding plumage, occasionally seen here, males have a red-brown back and a distinct black and white pattern on the head and neck. In the non-breeding plumage, these markings are more obscure and brownish. The legs are orange and the bill black. It usually occurs in single-species groups, or mixed flocks of small waders. Frequent on rocky coastlines, on sandy shores and mudflats, or open grassland. Turnstones occur throughout Seychelles, and are most abundant October–March, but some birds stay all year round.

Sanderling *Calidris alba*
Bekaso Blan | Wingspan 40–45cm | Migrant

A widespread annual migrant, most abundant here October–March. A small, plump wader with very pale plumage; light grey above, with white underparts and flanks. Common on sandy beaches, where it runs frantically along the sand just above the waterline, picking up invertebrates exposed by the backwash and running back up the beach to escape incoming waves. It also associates with other waders on mudflats in lagoons, etc.

Curlew Sandpiper *Calidris ferruginea*
Bekaso Korbizo | Wingspan 42–46cm | Migrant

A widespread annual migrant, abundant October–March. A small, slim wader with a down-curved bill. In flight, it exposes a white wingbar and rump. It is often seen in small feeding flocks on mudflats and in sandy shallows; these flocks sometimes include other small waders. At high tide, groups are often seen on short-cut lawns and airstrips.

Land Birds

Seychelles Kestrel *Falco araea*
Katiti | Wingspan 40–45cm | Endemic Resident
Breeds: granitics; Mahé and satellite islands, Silhouette, Praslin, North and Félicité

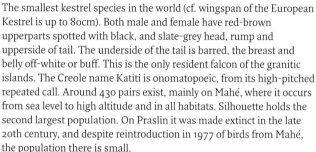

The smallest kestrel species in the world (cf. wingspan of the European Kestrel is up to 80cm). Both male and female have red-brown upperparts spotted with black, and slate-grey head, rump and upperside of tail. The underside of the tail is barred, the breast and belly off-white or buff. This is the only resident falcon of the granitic islands. The Creole name Katiti is onomatopoeic, from its high-pitched repeated call. Around 430 pairs exist, mainly on Mahé, where it occurs from sea level to high altitude and in all habitats. Silhouette holds the second largest population. On Praslin it was made extinct in the late 20th century, and despite reintroduction in 1977 of birds from Mahé, the population there is small.

The Seychelles Kestrel often associates with man, nesting in buildings as well as in palms, hollow trees and cliffs. Egg-laying occurs August–October. It feeds mainly on small vertebrates, such as *Phelsuma* geckos, and insects. The bird was once regarded with superstition as a bad omen, and has suffered persecution at the hands of humans. It is now protected by national law and international conventions.

Madagascar Kestrel *Falco newtoni*
Katiti Malgas | Wingspan 45–50cm | Native Resident
Breeds: Aldabra; Aldabra

A larger kestrel, with a brown-buff crown, white underside and belly spotted with black. Although not endemic to Seychelles, this kestrel has rather a restricted world range, occurring only in Madagascar and Aldabra. On Aldabra, its population is low, only around 50 pairs. It feeds on *Phelsuma* geckos and a range of other small vertebrate or invertebrate prey, and nests in palms, trees and buildings. The breeding season is August–January.

Grey Francolin *Francolinus pondicerianus*
Perdi | Wingspan 48–52cm | Introduced Resident
Breeds: corallines; Amirantes (Desroches), Coëtivy

Apart from the domestic chicken, which occurs in feral populations on many islands, this is the only resident gamebird in Seychelles. It was introduced to several of the coralline and granitic islands in the 19th century. Now it occurs only on Desroches and Coëtivy.

Aldabra Rail *Dryolimnas cuvieri aldabranus*

Tyomityo | length 30–32cm | Endemic Subspecies, Resident

Breeds: Aldabra; Aldabra

This rail, now confined to Aldabra although formerly found on most of the raised coralline islands of the Aldabra group, is the only surviving flightless bird in the western Indian Ocean. Predation by cats was probably a major factor in the loss of the Aldabra Rail from much of its former range which included Assumption, Cosmoledo and Astove. It has a generalist diet, sometimes following giant tortoises to eat the insects they disturb, and may also glean ectoparasites from the bodies of tortoises.

The Aldabra Rail is currently regarded as a subspecies of the White-throated Rail of Madagascar, which has larger wings and has retained its ability to fly. It is the only resident terrestrial rail in Seychelles. Found on the islands of Malabar, Picard, Polymnie and Île aux Cedres.

Malagasy Turtle Dove *Streptopelia picturata*

Toutrel Dezil | Wingspan 37–44cm (depending on race) | Endemic and Introduced Subspecies present, Resident

Breeds: granitics; all large and medium islands. *S. p. rostrata*-type on Aride, Cousin, Cousine | corallines: *S. p. rostrata*-type on Bird, *S. p. picturata* on Denis, Amirantes (D'Arros, St Joseph, Rémire) | Aldabra: *S. p. coppingeri* on Aldabra, ?Cosmoledo

A widespread large pigeon, mainly found in woodlands and gardens. While readily identifiable to species level – it is the only large pink-brown pigeon in Seychelles – the subspecific taxonomy of this species is complicated. It seems likely that at least three distinct races or subspecies occurred in different parts of Seychelles prior to human settlement. In the granitic islands, the small native variety *S. p. rostrata* had a dark purple head and blue-grey lower breast. The larger Amirantes subspecies *S. p. saturata* and the Aldabran subspecies *S. p. coppingeri* had dark purple-mauve head and pink-purple lower breast.

Following human settlement, the birds were persecuted, and a fourth variety of the same species, *S. p. picturata* from Madagascar, probably introduced. The Madagascar variety, now dominant in the granitic islands, is large with a distinctly grey head and purple-pink lower breast.

The native Amirantes form was driven to extinction by humans, although some of the Amirantes now have birds of the Madagascar race, probably introduced. On the granitic islands birds with characteristics of *S. p. rostrata* survive, but these are probably hybrid forms. The Aldabra form survives throughout Aldabra and on Cosmoledo (Cosmoledo birds may represent yet another island race).

Barred Ground, or Zebra, Dove *Geopelia striata*

Tourtrel Koko | Wingspan 25cm | Introduced Resident

Breeds: granitics; all large and medium islands | corallines: Bird, Denis, Coëtivy, Amirantes (D'Arros, St Joseph, Desroches), Farquhar group | Aldabra; Assumption

A small, long-tailed dove with generally grey plumage with fine dark bars. The breast often has a pink tinge, and the eye-ring and base of the bill are blue. The Barred Ground Dove, probably introduced as a cage bird, now occurs throughout the granitic islands, where its repetitive cooing call is familiar around habitation. It is also found on some of the Amirantes, Farquhar and Assumption (where it was introduced in 1976). Although present from sea level to high altitudes, the species thrives in open grassland and urban areas, where it feeds on tiny seeds and insects.

Aldabra Blue Pigeon *Alectroenas sganzini minor*

Pizon Olande Aldabra | Wingspan 36–40cm | Endemic Subspecies, Resident

Breeds: Aldabra; Aldabra

A fruit pigeon with pale blue/white breast, neck and head, and dark blue-black wings, belly and tail, and a red eye-ring. Only on Aldabra; other subspecies occur on Madagascar and Comores. The Blue Pigeon genus *Alectroenas* is only found on the islands of the Indian Ocean, with species on Madagascar, the Comores and Seychelles. There was previously a species on Mauritius, but this is now extinct. Most species feed on small, fleshy fruits.

Seychelles Blue Pigeon *Alectroenas pulcherrima*

Pizon Olande | Wingspan 39cm | Endemic Resident

Breeds: granitics; all large and medium islands | corallines; Denis

This fruit pigeon, endemic to the granitic islands, has a pale blue-white breast and neck, dark blue-black wings, belly and tail, and a red fleshy wattle around the eyes and a red cap. The Creole name is derived from the three colours of the pigeon, similar to those of the tricolor flag of the Netherlands. It is one of the more common endemic birds of Seychelles; populations were reduced by hunting in the past, but have expanded with the cessation of persecution, and it can now be seen throughout the granitic archipelago (and Denis, where it is probably introduced). It feeds on small to medium-sized fruit, such as the berries of *Canthium bibracteatum*, Cinnamon *Cinnamomum verum* and figs *Ficus* spp., which it swallows whole.

Rose-ringed, or Green, Parakeet *Psittacula krameri*

Kato Ver | Wingspan 42–48cm | Introduced Resident

Breeds: granitics; Mahé

This green, long-tailed parakeet – not to be confused with the now-extinct endemic Seychelles Parakeet *Psittacula eupatria wardi* – is a relatively recent introduction to Seychelles. Although occasional birds were recorded in the 1970s and 1980s on Mahé and Silhouette, it was not until the late 1990s that flocks were seen, the result of several distinct releases, some deliberate. Today, perhaps 50 individuals occur around Mahé in mobile flocks. They feed on fruit and seeds of a variety of trees. The Seychelles Ministry of Environment has announced its intention to cull these birds before they become fully established and cause ecological damage.

Seychelles Black Parrot *Coracopsis nigra*

Kato Nwanr | Wingspan 48–54cm | Native Resident

Breeds: granitics; Praslin, possibly Curieuse

Parrots thought to be the same species occur on Madagascar and the Comores, although the Seychelles' birds belong to a separate (endemic) subspecies (or possibly a separate species). It is one of the rarest endemic birds of the granitic islands, with a few hundred birds on Praslin; it is also seen on Curieuse. It feeds on fruit of native and introduced plants and can be encountered anywhere on Praslin, especially places with cultivated fruit trees such as Bilimbi *Averrhoa bilimbi* and Mango *Mangifera indica*. The Black Parrot flies in small flocks and has an unmistakeable call of high-pitched whistles (sometimes imitated by mynahs). Nests are built in hollow trees, a scarce and probably limiting resource on Praslin. A number of deep, rat-proof nestboxes have been erected for their use on Praslin and Curieuse.

Madagascar Coucal *Centropus toulou insularis*

Toulouz | Wingspan 41–47cm | Endemic Subspecies Resident

Breeds: Aldabra; Aldabra

A large, pheasant-like bird, with glossy black body and tail, and chestnut wings. Non-breeding individuals as pictured have duller plumage, and juveniles are mainly charcoal-grey with pale streaks on the head and neck, and red-brown wings. The Madagascar Coucal tends to skulk in dense woody vegetation and feeds on insects, lizards and small birds. Once found on Assumption and Cosmoledo, it is now restricted to Aldabra itself. The species is also found on Madagascar.

Barn Owl *Tyto alba*

Ibou | Wingspan 85–93cm | Introduced Resident

Breeds: granitics; all large to medium-sized islands, may 'commute' to smaller islands to feed

The Barn Owl is one of the most widespread birds in the world, absent only from polar regions and a few isolated islands, including (prior to 1949) Seychelles. It was deliberately introduced in 1949 and from 1951 onwards in an effort to control rats, and quickly spread through the granitic islands. While the bird does eat rats, it seems not to make a significant impact on the pest status of rodents, and also finds Fairy Terns easy prey. For many years, the Ministry of Environment operated a bounty system to try to control numbers, but the species is still fairly common, especially at lower and mid-altitudes. The birds introduced to Seychelles were of the East African race *Tyto alba affinis*, with rather orange underparts. This is the only large owl in Seychelles. It roosts in trees by day and is active by night, when it gives high-pitched shrieking calls. It used to occur (naturally) on Aldabra but is now extinct there.

Seychelles Scops Owl *Otus insularis*

Syer | Wingspan 40cm | Endemic Resident

Breeds: granitics; Mahé

The Seychelles Scops Owl is confined to Mahé, where it is largely restricted to forests at mid- or high altitudes in the north of the island, only rarely occurring below 200m. The world population is less than 360 birds. The Scops Owl is much smaller than the Barn Owl (Scops Owl height to 23cm, Barn Owl to 35cm). Its plumage is mottled dark grey-brown or reddish-brown. The bird has a distinctive call, a double frog-like croak that is supposed to resemble the sound of a saw – hence the Creole name, meaning sawyer – given from vantage points in tall trees. It feeds on invertebrates (spiders, beetles and crickets) and small lizards. Although several roads cross its range, this is a rarely seen bird, and a nest was not found until 1999. It nests in tree holes, probably mainly in endemic tree species. The European Scops Owl *Otus scops* is a rare vagrant in Seychelles.

Madagascar Nightjar *Caprimulgus madagascariensis*

Sonmey Malgas | Wingspan 35cm | Native Resident

Breeds: Aldabra; Aldabra

The only resident nightjar of Seychelles, where it is confined to Aldabra (the species also occurs on Madagascar). By day, it roosts on the ground, where its plumage provides excellent camouflage against shaded leaf litter and rocks. Active at night, when it catches its insect prey in flight. The Eurasian Nightjar *C. europaeus* has also been recorded as a vagrant in Seychelles.

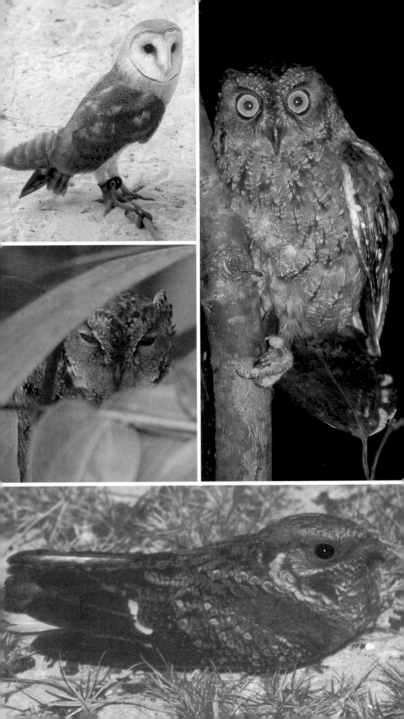

Seychelles Swiftlet   *Collocalia elapha (Aerodramus elaphrus)*
Zirondel | Wingspan 28cm | Endemic Resident
Breeds: granitics; Mahé, Praslin, La Digue

This is the only resident swift of Seychelles, although several other species may occur as vagrants. The Seychelles Swiftlet is a small all-dark fast-flying bird, relatively common on Mahé, Praslin and La Digue, and occasionally seen over other granitic islands. It breeds communally in caves, generally over 150m in altitude. Inside the cave, the birds rely on echolocation for navigation. The nests are cup-shaped and constructed of plant material such as mosses or leaf fragments cemented with saliva. Only a few breeding sites are known. The Swiftlet feeds in flocks, catching small insects on the wing. The total population is 2,500–3,000 birds.

Red-whiskered Bulbul   *Pycnonotus jocosus*
Merl Konde | Wingspan 23cm | Introduced Resident
Breeds: Aldabra; Assumption

An attractive and noisy bulbul species frequently kept as a cage bird in its native South-east Asia and introduced to Assumption in 1976. By 1997, the population exceeded 1,000 birds. This adaptable generalist now threatens to colonise Aldabra, where it could pose a threat in ecosystems otherwise free of introduced birds.

Seychelles Bulbul   *Hypsipetes crassirostris*
Merl | Wingspan 36cm | Endemic Resident
Breeds: granitics; La Digue, Mahé, Praslin, Silhouette (and a few satellite islands)

A dark brown bulbul with orange bill and legs, and an untidy black crest. Juveniles have dull-coloured bill and legs and red-brown flight feathers. This is one of the more common endemic birds of Seychelles, although it is confined to the four large granitic islands and a few close satellite islands. It occurs in woodland and gardens from sea level to the highest altitudes and has a broad diet, eating fruit, invertebrates and small vertebrates. A gregarious, noisy species, aggressive and easily detected by its loud cackling and bubbling calls. Breeds mainly October–January.

Madagascar Bulbul   *Hypsipetes madagascariensis*
Merl Malgas | Wingspan 36cm | Native Resident
Breeds: Aldabra; Aldabra

A dark grey-brown bulbul with orange bill and brown legs. This widespread species occurs (as different races) from Madagascar to South-east Asia. In Seychelles, it was formerly found on Aldabra, Cosmoledo and Astove but is now confined to Aldabra, where an endemic race *H. m. rostratus* is relatively abundant (up to 8,000 pairs estimated). It has a broad diet, including insects, fruit, seeds and flowers.

Seychelles Magpie Robin   *Copsychus sechellarum*

Pi Santez | Wingspan 29cm | Endemic Resident
Breeds: granitics; Aride, Cousin, Cousine, Frégate

This attractive black and white bird, with a beautiful song, is now the rarest endemic bird of Seychelles, with around 120 individuals on four islands. At its rarest, in 1970, it was reduced to about 25 individuals on just one island, Frégate. Only the implementation of an active conservation programme, beginning with the eradication of cats on Frégate and continuing with the translocation of some birds to other predator-free islands, has prevented its complete extinction. While it was once widespread in the granitic archipelago, it was vulnerable to competition and predation by a range of introduced predators, and was caught as a cage bird.

The Magpie Robin is a species of lowland woodland and gardens, feeding largely on invertebrates from leaf litter on the woodland floor as well as fish dropped by seabirds, and small reptiles. It sometimes forages around Giant Tortoises that disturb invertebrates as they walk; on Cousin and Aride, it uses human visitors in the same way. It nests in trees and Coconut Palms (and now nestboxes); mynahs have been identified as a competitor for nest sites, and are controlled on Frégate.

Male and female are alike in plumage, although that of the juvenile bird is less glossy and shows less contrast; the white wing feathers are edged with cinnamon brown.

Seychelles Warbler   *Acrocephalus sechellensis*

Timerl Dezil | Wingspan 17cm | Endemic Resident
Breeds: granitics; Aride, Cousin, Cousine

A rather drab endemic warbler, generally olive-brown to grey in colour with paler yellowish underparts. This is the only resident warbler of the granitic Seychelles and is found only on a few predator-free islands; Cousin, Cousine and Aride (also recently introduced to Denis). It reached a population-low of less than 30 birds, all on Cousin, in the 1960s; but today, following an active conservation programme, the population is approximately 3,000. A great deal of research has been carried out on this species, which has revealed that the bird has a variety of strategies for coping with life on small islands. Young adults often stay at the nest helping to raise their parent's young, while waiting for breeding opportunities themselves, and the sex ratio of offspring is governed by the environment.

Seychelles Paradise Flycatcher *Terspiphone corvina*

Vev | Wingspan 23cm | Endemic Resident

Breeds: granitics; La Digue

A beautiful small bird now restricted to La Digue, though birds are occasionally seen on the nearby islands of Félicité and Marianne. The world population is less than 300 birds. Males are glossy black with very long tail streamers (to 22cm), and bright blue eye-ring and bill. Females and juveniles have a black head, white belly and chestnut upperparts and tail. The Creole name Vev (widow) refers to the male plumage. Flycatchers feed on insects and spiders, caught on the wing or gleaned from the undersides of leaves. On La Digue, they are most abundant in the tall, native woodland of the plateau. A small patch of damp woodland and adjacent marshes is maintained as the Vev Reserve, for their protection, but they can be found wherever there is native or mixed woodland. The birds build a small cup-shaped nest at the tips of thin branches of broadleaved trees. Breeding takes place all year round, with a distinct peak in the North-west Monsoon (November–March).

Souimanga Sunbird *Nectarinia sovimanga*

Kolibri Aldabra | Wingspan 13cm | Endemic Subspecies Resident

Breeds: Aldabra; Aldabra

A small, brightly coloured bird with a narrow, hooked bill, used for feeding on nectar and small invertebrates. This species is found in Madagascar and Aldabra (where there is an endemic race *N. s. aldabrensis*). The similar Abbott's Sunbird (*N. s. abbotti*, or *N. abbotti*) is found on Assumption, Astove and Cosmoledo.

Seychelles Sunbird *Nectarinia dussumieri*

Kolibri | Wingspan 16cm | Endemic Resident

Breeds: granitics; almost all islands

The Seychelles Sunbird lacks the bright plumage of many of its relatives, although males have a metallic dark purple bib and orange tufts of feathers beneath the wing (usually invisible when the bird is at rest). It occurs on almost all the large, medium-sized and many small granitic islands, and can be found in a range of habitats including woodland, scrub and gardens from sea level to the highest peaks. It feeds on invertebrates and nectar. Pairs are very territorial and males have an exceptionally loud call for such a small bird. Breeding occurs year-round but peaks in September–October. The nest is a beautifully woven hanging structure made of leaves, moss and spiders' webs.

Madagascar White-eye *Zosterops maderaspatana*
Zwazo Linet Malgas | Wingspan 14cm | Endemic Subspecies Resident
Breeds: Aldabra; Aldabra, Astove, Cosmoledo

White-eyes are small, often yellowish or grey birds with a white eye-ring. Endemic species are found on many of the islands of the Indian Ocean and around Africa. This species is found on Aldabra, Astove and Cosmoledo, with endemic races in each location. It is the only species of white-eye on the raised coralline islands. It occurs in small flocks, moving through vegetation to feed on insects.

Seychelles White-eye *Zosterops modestus*
Zwazo Linet | Wingspan 15cm | Endemic Resident
Breeds: granitics; Concéption, Mahé, Frégate

The Seychelles White-eye has grey plumage and a barely visible white eye-ring. It is the only white-eye in the granitic islands. Until 1997, it was believed to be one of the rarest of the Seychelles' endemic birds, only known from a few locations on Mahé including gardens and forest at La Misère, Cascade and a few other places. In 1997, a thriving population of 250 or more was discovered on Concéption, off the west coast of Mahé. This population has been used as the basis for translocation to Frégate island, where the bird is doing well. The white-eye is largely a forest bird, although it does not require native woodland and survives well in species-poor Cinnamon forest. It eats insects and small fruit, including the fruit of Lantana and Cinnamon.

Aldabra Drongo *Dicrurus aldabrensis*
Moulanba | Wingspan 34cm | Endemic Resident
Breeds: Aldabra; Aldabra

A glossy black, medium-sized bird with a long, forked tail. Endemic to Aldabra. The Drongo is insectivorous and can be seen among trees, mangroves or scrub. There may be 500 pairs of this bird on Aldabra and although it has a very restricted world range, it is not regarded as in imminent danger of extinction – it is listed as 'near threatened'.

Pied Crow *Corvus alba*

Korbo Blan e Nwanr | Wingspan 100cm | ?Native Resident
Breeds: Aldabra; Aldabra, Assumption, Astove, Cosmoledo

Pied Crows scavenge on beaches and around settlements on islands in the Aldabra group and nowhere else in Seychelles. Elsewhere, the species occurs throughout southern and eastern Africa, Madagascar and the Comores. There is some dispute as to whether it is native, or an early introduction by man. It feeds opportunistically on small vertebrates including turtle hatchlings and on birds' eggs, carrion and human rubbish. Pied Crows occur in quite low numbers in Seychelles; there are probably less than 100 birds on Aldabra.

Common, or Indian, Mynah *Acridotheres tristis*

Marten | Wingspan 35cm | Introduced Resident
Breeds: granitics; almost all islands | corallines: Bird, Denis

This noisy, aggressive, introduced starling is found throughout the inner islands in a wide range of habitats from sea level to the highest peaks. It is an omnivorous opportunist, feeding on fruit and nectar, insects, crabs, small vertebrates and rubbish. The plumage is dark brown with large white patches in the wings, especially visible in flight. Some individuals called 'king mynahs' have featherless, yellow heads.

Mynahs gather in huge flocks at roost trees around dusk. They nest in palms, trees, house roofs and nestboxes provided for other birds. Mynahs have been spread throughout the world from their original range in South and South-east Asia. Where introduced, they have often become pests; in Seychelles, they compete with endemic birds for nest sites, and may eat their eggs and nestlings.

Common Waxbill *Estrilda astrild*

Bengali | Wingspan 13cm | Introduced Resident
Breeds: granitics; Mahé, La Digue | corallines; Amirantes (Alphonse)

A small African finch species found on Mahé, La Digue and Alphonse. Seen in small flocks in gardens, scrub and roadside habitats, often feeding on the seeds of grasses. The Common Waxbill builds a relatively large domed nest in shrubs and grasses.

House Sparrow *Passer domesticus*

Mwano | Wingspan 21–25cm | Introduced Resident
Breeds: granitics; ?Mahé | corallines; Amirantes (D'Arros, St Joseph, Rémire, Desroches, Desnoeufs, Marie-Louise, Alphonse, Bijoutier, St François)

One of the most widely distributed birds in the world. In Seychelles, it is established on some of the Amirantes and Alphonse islands. A small, newly established population on Mahé was eradicated in 2003 but there is the continual threat of reinvasion on container ships.

Madagascar Fody *Foudia madagascariensis*
Kardinal | Wingspan 18cm | Introduced Resident
Breeds: granitics; almost all islands | corallines; Bird, Denis, Platte, Amirantes (Rémire, D'Arros, St Joseph, Desroches), Farquhar group | Aldabra; Assumption

This is a common and widespread introduced land bird. In breeding condition, mainly September–April in the granitic group, males are bright orange-red with a black mask and dark wings. Outside the breeding season, males moult to become mid-brown in colour, usually retaining some patches of red. In a few birds, the red coloration is replaced by bright yellow. Females are brown all year round. This species, originally a Madagascar endemic, has been extensively introduced outside its natural range. In Seychelles, it is highly successful, exploiting open habitats around settlements, as well as natural glacis and scrub. Its diet consists mainly of seeds of grasses and *Casuarina*. It builds a woven nest suspended from vegetation, protecting the eggs and chicks from predation. It is found throughout the granitic islands, on the Amirantes and Assumption, but not on Aldabra itself.

Seychelles Fody *Foudia sechellarum*
Toktok | Wingspan 18cm | Endemic Resident
Breeds: granitics; Aride, Cousin, Cousine, Frégate | corallines; Amirantes (D'Arros), Denis

The Seychelles Fody resembles a darker, stockier and larger version of the female Madagascar Fody; it is greenish brown, with darker streaks on the wings and back and (usually) a pale spot on the edge of each wing. In breeding plumage, the male has a small patch of bright yellow feathers around the bill (*see* photo).

Generally, the Seychelles Fody prefers areas with dense vegetation cover. Natural populations survived on Cousin, Cousine and Frégate, despite the islands' conversion to coconut plantations, perhaps because of the absence of introduced predators. The regeneration of native forest on these islands has favoured the species. Its broad diet includes insects, seeds, fruit and (in season) seabird eggs.

Although regarded as a globally threatened bird, the world population has increased and there are now at least 3,000 individuals.

Aldabra Fody *Foudia eminentissima aldabrana*
Kardinal Aldabra | Wingspan 22cm | Endemic Subspecies Resident
Breeds: Aldabra; Aldabra

A large fody found only on Aldabra. The breeding male (as pictured) has a red head and breast, and yellow belly. The breeding season lasts October–April and after this, the male loses much of his red coloration. The female is brown. The Aldabra Fody feeds on seeds, especially those of *Casuarina* trees, and insects. The hanging woven nest is usually built in Coconut Palms or shrubs.

Reptiles

When the islands of the granitic Seychelles were first discovered by humans, the largest land animal was a crocodilian, the Estuarine (or Saltwater) Crocodile *Crocodylus porosus*. This species, which survives today in Asia and Australasia, is the world's largest living reptile, reaching a length of 6.5m or more, and is one of the most dangerous to man. However, within about 50 years of the founding of the Seychelles' colony in 1770, the 'Caiman' was extinct here. Seychelles is several thousand kilometres outside its current range.

Following the extinction of the crocodile, another reptile, the giant tortoise, was the largest surviving land animal of Seychelles. Giant tortoises were, at that time, found on almost all the granitic islands and Denis as well as the Aldabra group, Farquhar, and possibly other coralline islands. Several 'endemic' species were described from the granitic islands on the basis of their shell shapes and general appearance, but few specimens were collected before the tortoises of the granitic islands followed the crocodile to extinction, due to the combined effects of hunting of adults and the loss of nests and hatchlings to introduced predators. Tortoises survived only on Aldabra, and even on that remote atoll there was concern for the survival of the species due to over-exploitation in the 19th century. Recent genetic work suggests that the tortoises of the inner islands were the same species as those of Aldabra, which survive today. Aldabra Giant Tortoises have been re-introduced quite successfully to some of the granitic islands. Seychelles now holds one of only two surviving giant tortoise species in the world – the other is on Galapagos.

The smaller reptiles of Seychelles have fared better than these giants, although one freshwater terrapin may be extinct and at least one lizard species, the Wright's Skink, appears unable to survive alongside rats and cats and is restricted to predator-free islands. Humans have been responsible for the introduction of several reptile species, although many of these are restricted to man-made habitats and have had little impact on native reptiles. Today, Seychelles has about 30 species of land reptile, including the giant tortoise, marine turtles, terrapins, snakes, and lizards.

Tortoises and Turtles

Seychelles has only one species of giant tortoise, at least two species of freshwater terrapin (restricted to the granitic islands) and two sea turtles that breed throughout the archipelago, especially on less-disturbed or predator-free islands.

OPPOSITE: Giant Tortoise.

Aldabra Giant Tortoise *Aldabrachelys elephantina* (*A. dussumieri,*
Dipsochelys dussumieri, Geochelone gigantea)

Torti-d-ter | Length (carapace) to 1m | Endemic

Found: granitics; Curieuse, Frégate, North, Cousin, Cousine (re-introduced populations)
and widespread in captivity | Corallines; Bird (introduced population | Aldabra; Aldabra
(wild population)

Giant tortoises were once found on many of the islands of the Indian
Ocean including Madagascar, the Comores, Farquhar, the Aldabra group
and the granitic Seychelles. Colonisation probably occurred as adult
tortoises (*a*) were carried between islands on ocean currents – tortoises
may enter the sea to cool themselves, especially where there is little fresh
water; they float (*b*), and can survive for some time without feeding.

Prior to human arrival, tortoises were found on most of the granitic
islands and Denis, as well as Providence, St Pierre, Aldabra, Astove,
Assumption and Cosmoledo. Several species were named but recent
genetic analysis suggests that they were the same as the surviving
Aldabra species, which also probably once occurred in northern
Madagascar (the correct name of the species is debateable – *see* the list
of synonyms above).

As humans discovered the islands, they hunted the adults for food
and introduced predators that destroyed their eggs and killed young
tortoises (*c*). It seems that all the giant tortoises of the Indian Ocean
were wiped out, with the exception of the animals on Aldabra atoll.

Aldabra still supports the largest wild population of giant tortoises in
the region. Due to the harshness of the terrain, numbers vary widely,
with 130,000 animals in the 1970s; now there are around 100,000.
Tortoises feed mainly on vegetation, particularly low grasses,
maintaining a characteristic species-rich 'tortoise turf' in locations where
grazing pressure is greatest (for example, eastern Grand Terre). In the
heat of the day, they seek shelter under bushes or in shallow pools.
Mating takes place mainly during the North-west Monsoon. The male
has a concave plastron (underside of the shell) to allow him to mount the
female. The peak nesting period is June–September; females dig nests in
soil in slightly shaded places and the eggs take two to five months to
hatch. Rats and birds are important predators of the hatchlings. If they
survive their early years, tortoises may be very long-lived and have little
to fear from predators. Tortoises are capable of growth throughout their
life, if conditions permit. In captivity, giant tortoises can live for over 150
years. The largest individual in Seychelles is reputed to be Esmerelda
(a male) on Bird Island, which weighed 304kg in 1995.

Tortoises have been introduced to various islands and there are now
sizable free-roaming, breeding populations (each over 200 individuals)
on Curieuse and Frégate. They are also widely kept in captivity.

Green Turtle *Chelonia mydas*

Torti-d-Mer | Length (carapace) to 1.4m | Native

Breeds: granitics; most islands, rarely | corallines; all islands | Aldabra; all islands

Although the Green Turtle has a wide distribution in the warm seas of the world, it is regarded as globally endangered as it is hunted wherever it occurs for its edible flesh, and nesting beaches are vulnerable to disturbance. The Green Turtle is usually olive-brown in colour; it derives its name from the colour of its fat. It breeds on beaches mainly on Aldabra and the remote southern islands, although each year a few nest on islands in the granitic archipelago, including Bird and Denis. Nesting occurs year-round, with two peaks: one January–April and one in July–September. Adult females, their carapaces up to 1.4m long, come up the beach at night to lay their eggs. The nests are about 80cm deep and are dug in sand at the beach crest, and over 100 eggs laid. Hatching occurs two months later, usually at night. Hatchlings are vulnerable to a range of predators including ghost crabs. They are also easily confused by beach lighting, which can cause them to head inland rather than out to sea. Young turtles are probably omnivorous, but adults feed almost exclusively on seagrasses and algae.

Hawksbill Turtle *Eretmochelys imbricate*

Kare | Length (carapace) to 95cm | Native

Breeds: granitics; all islands, most successfully on reserve islands | corallines; most islands | Aldabra; all islands

The Hawksbill is the commonest turtle found around the granitic islands, but globally it is considered 'Critically Endangered' (IUCN Red List). It is smaller than the Green Turtle, the carapace rarely exceeding 95cm in length, and is usually yellow and brown. While it is occasionally taken for food, its flesh can be poisonous; it is omnivorous – feeding on sponges, other invertebrates and algae – and sometimes toxins from its prey concentrate in its own flesh. The Hawksbill breeds on beaches throughout Seychelles, including even the busy island of Mahé. The peak breeding season is during the North-west Monsoon, particularly mid-October–mid-January, and during this time females come ashore to dig nest holes at the beach crest. The eggs hatch after two months; young turtles emerge at or after dusk and head down the beach to the sea. The Hawksbill has been hunted in the past for tortoiseshell, but both this species and the Green Turtle are now protected by international treaty and by Seychelles law.

Several other turtles are occasionally seen in the western Indian Ocean but do not breed here – including the Leathery or Leatherback Turtle *Dermochelys coriacea* and the Loggerhead Turtle *Caretta caretta*.

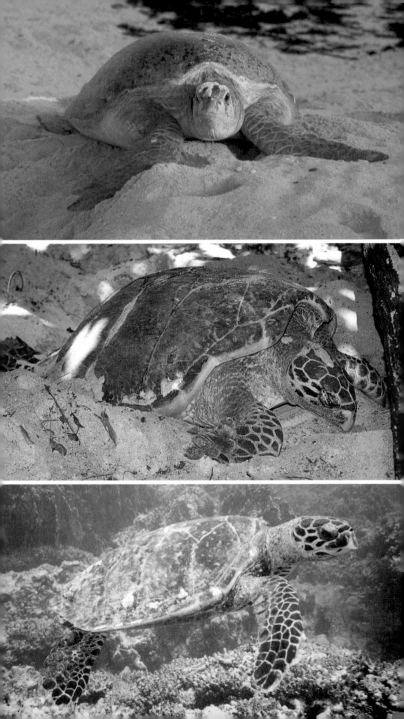

Pelusios *(Torti Soupap or Hinged Terrapins)*

Three terrapins of the genus *Pelusios* have been recorded in Seychelles, although one of these, the endemic species *Pelusios seychellensis*, is probably extinct. The two surviving species are both represented by endemic subspecies; different forms of the same species occur in East Africa and Madagascar. They are rather similar in appearance, and both have a hinge on the underside of the shell (the plastron) that allows them to withdraw the head and forelimbs, closing the shell for protection. Both species feed in the water, eating invertebrates, fish and fruits; if their marshes dry out, they take refuge in damp mud. The *Pelusios* species can be differentiated most reliably by details of the shell structure and head scalation. However, the simplest way to tell them apart is by the colour of the carapace and plastron (*see* below). A third (introduced) species of terrapin occurs in Seychelles. It lacks the hinged plastron of *Pelusios* species.

Seychelles Black Mud Terrapin   *Pelusios subniger parietalis*

Torti Soupap | Length (carapace) to 20cm | Native (Endemic Subspecies)
Found: granitics; Mahé, La Digue, Cerf, Frégate, Cousin, possibly other islands

The upper shell (carapace) of this species is a uniform dark grey-brown, and the plastron yellow-grey, with black patches, which are sometimes extensive. The skin of the neck and limbs is grey or black.

Seychelles Yellow-bellied Mud Terrapin
Pelusios castanoides intergularis

Torti Soupap | Length (carapace) to 23cm | Native (Endemic Subspecies)
Found: granitics; Mahé, Praslin, La Digue, Cerf, possibly other islands

The carapace of this species is often yellow-brown in older individuals, although it may be olive or dark brown in younger animals. The plastron is yellow, sometimes with dark suture lines but always lacking extensive symmetrical patches of black. The skin of the neck and limbs is yellowish.

Red-eared Terrapin or Red-eared Slider   *Trachemys scripta elegans*

Length (carapace) to 28cm | Introduced
Found: granitics; Mahé

A terrapin originating from North America. Hatchlings are sold as pets throughout the world and individuals have been imported (illegally) to Seychelles several times in recent years. Pet animals tend to outgrow their welcome and may be released into the wild, and it is possible that an ecologically damaging breeding population could be established in the future. Young Red-eared Terrapins are brightly coloured and attractive. Their limbs and carapace are striped in shades of green and yellow and they have a red mark on each side of the head. Adults become predominantly drab olive-brown to black.

Snakes

There are three species of snake in Seychelles, two of which are endemic to the granitic group, where they occur on the larger islands. The third species, a small burrowing snake, is introduced and is widespread (though rarely seen), occurring on some small islands in the granitic group as well as some of the coralline islands. Aldabra has no snakes.

Seychelles Wolf Snake   *Lycognathophis seychellensis*

Koulev | Length 1.3m | Endemic

Found: granitics; Mahé, Praslin, Silhouette, La Digue, Frégate, Aride, Cousine

This is the most commonly seen snake of Seychelles, due to its wide occurrence on the larger granitic islands and its diurnal habits. It is a thin-bodied, fast-moving snake that occurs in two main colour forms: one is dark brown, often with a few scattered golden scales (*a*), while the other is predominantly golden brown (*b*). Solitary individuals may be seen especially in mid-altitude forests, and the animal is often disturbed on little-used forest tracks. It moves away rapidly when disturbed and is completely harmless.

Seychelles House Snake   *Boaedon geometricus*

Koulev | Length 1.2m | Endemic

Found: granitics; Mahé, Praslin, Silhouette, Frégate

The Seychelles House Snake is primarily nocturnal, although it may occasionally be seen in the late afternoon. It can reach 1.2m in length (usually less) and is much thicker-bodied than the Wolf Snake. Despite its name, it is not usually found around human habitation, preferring woodland, scrub and plantation, and is much less frequently encountered than the Wolf Snake. It is mid-brown in colour with longitudinal darker stripes along its body and shows purple iridescence in good light. Because of its bulk, it can take larger prey than the Wolf Snake and can bite humans, although its bite is not dangerous.

Lizards

Family Chamaeleonidae – Chameleons
An entirely Old World (predominantly African) lizard family, with one representative in Seychelles.

Tiger Chameleon   *Calumma tigris* (*Chameleo tigris*)
Kameleon | Length to 20cm | Endemic
Breeds: granitics; Mahé, Praslin, Silhouette

This, the only chameleon in Seychelles, is an unusual lizard with independently moving eyes and two toes on each foot. It feeds on small insects caught with its long tongue. The chameleon spends much of its life climbing in vegetation, but may occasionally be seen on the ground, for example crossing roads, where it is slow-moving and vulnerable. The markings are often bright yellow and black, but vary through a range of grey and moss-green tones. It can be seen on the larger granitic islands, in a variety of wooded or scrubby habitats from sea level to higher altitudes (500m or more).

Family Agamidae – Agamids
A family of lizards similar to the iguanas of the New World. In Seychelles, only one recently introduced species occurs.

Tree Dragon, Crested Dragon, Changeable Lizard or Bloodsucker   *Calotes versicolor*
Length to 37cm | Introduced
Found: granitics; Ste Anne, Mahé

This large, active lizard originates in South and South-East Asia, from India to southern China and Thailand. It has been widely introduced around the world, either deliberately or accidentally. In Seychelles, it probably arrived in the late 1990s with cargo from Mauritius, where it is common in lowland habitats. It is an agile climber and effective predator, feeding on invertebrates, other lizards and small birds. There seems to be a well-established population on Sainte Anne and it probably also breeds on Mahé.

Family Scincidae – Skinks

A large family of elongate, active lizards. Most can shed their tails as a defence against predators. In Seychelles, there are five species.

Wright's Skink *Mabuya wrightii*

Teng Teng | Length to 33cm | Endemic

Found: granitics; predator-free islands including Aride, Cousin, Cousine, Frégate and some smaller islets

This large, bulky skink appears unable to survive alongside introduced predators, and is today restricted to a few predator-free islands in the granitic Seychelles that are also the home of large seabird colonies. Here, they occur at high densities on the forest floor – up to 1,300 individuals per hectare. They feed on dropped fish and squid, fallen seabird eggs and chicks, other skinks, insects, fruit and food scraps.

Seychelles Skink *Mabuya sechellensis*

Lezar Mangouya | Length to 23cm | Endemic

Found: granitics; almost all islands | corallines; Bird, Denis, Amirantes (D'Arros, St Joseph, Rémire)

This smaller, slimmer skink species has a distinct black stripe along its side. In contrast, the sides of theWright's Skink are mid-brown, with a chequered appearance. The Seychelles Skink is found on almost all islands in the granitic group, and some coral islands. The Seychelles Skink is an efficient climber, clambering up Coconut stems and trees to a height of several metres. It occurs in woodland, plantations, gardens and houses from sea level to mid-altitudes. It lays its paired eggs underground.

Burrowing Skink *Pamelaescincus gardineri*

Lezar Later | Length 12–15cm | Endemic

Found: granitics; Mahé, Praslin, Silhouette, La Digue, Curieuse, Félicité, Frégate, Aride, Cousin and other small islands

A small, elongate skink with rather reduced limbs. It occurs in forest habitat from sea level to mid-altitudes on many islands, but is rarely seen, as it burrows in leaf litter and soil. Diurnal on Praslin, nocturnal on other islands. The similar, related species *Janetaescincus braueri* is found on Mahé, Silhouette and Frégate.

Bouton's Skink *Cryptoblepharus boutonii* (*Ablepharus boutonii*)

Lezar | Length to 10cm | Native

Found: corallines; Farquhar (Farquhar, Providence, St Pierre) | Aldabra; Aldabra, Cosmoledo, Assumption and Astove

A small, slim skink found on the raised coralline islands and the Farquhar group, where it is the only skink species. It occurs throughout the Indo-Pacific region. Found in a range of habitats. It feeds on land invertebrates, crustaceans and sometimes fish.

Family Gekkonidae – Geckos

A family of small to medium-sized lizards remarkable for their ability to climb vertical surfaces and ceilings, using pads on the underside of their toes. Many have the ability to shed their tails or patches of skin to escape predators. Most lay paired eggs, which are attached to rough surfaces.

Pacific House Gecko *Gehyra mutilata*

Lezar Disik | Length 10cm | Introduced

Found: granitics; all inhabited islands | corallines; Denis, Coëtivy, Farquhar group, occasionally transported to other corallines | Aldabra; ?Aldabra (recorded but perhaps not established)

The common house gecko of the granitic islands, also occurring on Denis, Farquhar, Coëtivy and possibly other coralline islands. This is a pale, nocturnal lizard that gathers around lights to feed on moths, beetles and smaller geckos. On some islands, it is also found in coconut plantations. *Gehyra* differs from the other house geckos (genus *Hemidactylus*) in its smooth dorsal surface and the broad, flattened base of its tail. It has a relatively quiet call.

Asian House Gecko *Hemidactylus frenatus*

Lezar Disik | Length to 13.5cm | ?Introduced

Found: granitics; Mahé | corallines; Bird, Platte, Amirantes (Desroches, Desnoeufs, Poivre, D'Arros, Rémire, Alphonse)

The only house gecko on several of the coralline islands, including Bird and many of the Amirantes. It also occurs on Mahé, where it is scarce and may be a recent colonist. Its dorsal surface is usually greyish or pink-brown with darker speckles and the tail has rings of raised tubercles along its length. The call consists of several very loud chirps, one after another. It is a nocturnal species that feeds around lights in buildings, or (sometimes) in natural habitats. Another Asian *Hemidactylus* gecko, *H. brookii* (introduced) occurs only on Desroches.

Sucker-tailed Gecko *Urocotyledon inexpectata*

Lezar Disik | Length 8cm | Endemic

Found: granitics; Mahé, Praslin, Silhouette, La Digue, Curieuse, Félicité, Frégate, Grande Soeur, Aride

A small endemic gecko, with heart-shaped pads at the tips of its toes and an adhesive sucker at the end of its tail. Found in natural woodland habitats and sometimes in houses, from sea level to mid-altitudes. This gecko seems relatively widespread in the granitic islands, but is rarely seen as it is small, cryptic and largely nocturnal.

AILURONYX SPP.

Bronze-eyed Geckos

Endemic

Ailuronyx seychellensis | max 20cm (snout–vent length 8–12cm) | Mahé, Praslin, Silhouette, La Digue, Curieuse, Félicité, Frégate, Aride, Cousin, Cousine

Ailuronyx tachyscopaeus | max 15cm (snout–vent length 6–8cm) | Mahé, Silhouette, Praslin, La Digue, Concéption

Ailuronyx trachygaster | max 15cm | Praslin, Silhouette

 The Bronze-eyed Gecko genus *Ailuronyx* is endemic to the granitic Seychelles. All are rather bulky arboreal geckos with warty skin patterned in pale yellow-brown, dark brown and grey, and with metallic gold eyes; while the markings are often pale–mid-brown, they may be more uniformly dark or show heightened contrast. The three species can be distinguished by size and distribution. On the larger granitic islands they survive alongside introduced mammals in woodland habitats, but at lower densities than on the predator-free islands. They feed on nectar, insects, carrion and (on seabird islands) seabirds' eggs. As a defence against predation, they can shed pieces of skin. The large eggs are usually laid in pairs attached to vegetation.

***PHELSUMA* GECKOS** *Phelsuma* geckos are brightly coloured and diurnal, and occur in a wide range of habitats including coconut plantations. The granitic Seychelles has at least two species, *P. astriata* and *P. sundbergi*. A third form is sometimes recognised as a full species (*P. longinsulae*), sometimes as a subspecies of *P. sundbergi*. *Phelsuma* survive on most of the granitic islands except for the very smallest. Two further native species are found on southern coralline islands and raised atolls. All feed on invertebrates and nectar and pollen produced by palms.

Green, or Day, Gecko *Phelsuma astriata*

Lezar Ver | Length 12–13cm | Endemic

Found: granitics; all islands | corallines; Denis, Amirantes (D'Arros, St Joseph) | Aldabra; Astove

 A small green gecko with white belly and green or yellow-green eye-ring. The dorsal side has irregular red markings, usually including a red chevron on the head between the eyes and two narrow transverse red bars on the neck. There is often a narrow red line and scattered red spots on the back, and narrow red bars or spots on the upperside of the tail. The most widespread green gecko species, occurring on almost all the inner islands (often alongside *P. longinsulae* or *P. sundbergi*), and several coralline islands, where it may have been introduced. On Mahé, Silhouette, Frégate and Astove, the subspecies *P. astriata astriata* occurs; the form on Praslin and La Digue, as well as Denis, D'Arros and St Joseph, is *P. a. semicarinata* (pictured).

Green, or Day, Gecko *Phelsuma longinsulae*
(*Phelsuma sundbergi longinsulae*)

Lezar Ver | Length 12–14cm | Endemic

Found: granitics; Mahé and satellites, Silhouette, Frégate, North | corallines; Bird, Amirantes (Rémire) | Aldabra; Cosmoledo

This species is absent from the Praslin group. On the Mahé group, it occurs alongside *P. astriata* and is similar to that species in size. The dorsum is green with red spots in one to three longitudinal rows. There is usually a red chevron between the eyes and a red line from the nostril to the eye. The eye-ring is yellow and there is a dark chevron on the chin, absent in *P. astriata*.

Green, or Day, Gecko *Phelsuma sundbergi*

Lezar Ver | Length 19cm | Endemic

Found: granitics; Praslin, La Digue, Curieuse, Félicité, Marianne, Les Soeurs, Île Cocos | corallines; Denis, Platte, Amirantes (Marie-Louise, Poivre)

The largest green gecko species in the granitic Seychelles, *P. sundbergi* is predominantly bright green to turquoise in colour. Some individuals show a varying amount of red on their dorsal surface – usually a smattering of small red freckles, sometimes none. The eye-ring is typically green to yellow-green. Found in palm forest and coconut plantations on granitic islands in the Praslin group, also Denis and a few other coralline islands.

Green, or Day, Gecko *Phelsuma abbotti*

Lezar Ver | Length 10–15cm | Native (two Endemic Subspecies)

Found: Aldabra; Aldabra, Assumption

This species occurs in Madagascar, Aldabra and Assumption, with endemic subspecies in each of these locations. On Aldabra, the sub-species *P. a. abbotti* (pictured) is found on the islands of Malabar, Taka-maka and Picard. It has a greenish-grey back, with flanks mottled blue-grey, a whitish eye-ring and white belly. The Assumption subspecies is larger, predominantly grey to bright blue with an interrupted red dorsal line and other scattered red markings, and a yellow-orange belly. It occurs on Coconut Palms and (on Aldabra) in association with tortoises.

Family Gerrhosauridae – Plated Lizards

Madagascar Plated Lizard *Zonosaurus madagascariensis*

Length 45cm | Native

Found: Aldabra; Cosmoledo

This large, mainly ground-dwelling lizard, resembling a giant skink, is found on Cosmoledo as well as the Glorieuses islands and Madagascar itself. The Cosmoledo and Glorieuses lizards have been described as a separate subspecies from the Madagascar form.

Amphibians

Most amphibian species have thin skin, which they use for oxygen exchange and must be kept damp at all times. Their eggs lack the hard shell of reptile or bird eggs and many species (though by no means all) lay their eggs in water. These features tend to limit the kind of habitats in which amphibians are found; few can survive in salty water or dry places. As a result, amphibians are absent from most oceanic islands, unable to cross extensive seawater barriers or survive the seasonally dry conditions there.

However, the granitic Seychelles is unusual among oceanic island groups as it was once connected to a continent. As a result, it has quite a large amphibian fauna (13 species) consisting of animals whose ancestors never had to cross a water barrier, or did so when the distance to the 'mainland' was much less. The antiquity of the Seychelles' amphibian fauna is demonstrated in its high endemicity; 12 of the 13 species are found nowhere else on earth, and the only non-endemic species may have been introduced by man.

Seven of Seychelles' amphibian species belong to the order Gymnophiona, the caecilians – they might be mistaken for large worms. Six are frogs, and four of these belong to the endemic family Sooglossidae.

None of the coralline islands or raised coralline atolls of Seychelles support any amphibians.

Caecilians

Caecilians are limbless amphibians with long, wormlike, segmented bodies. They have much reduced eyes, no ear openings and a pair of tiny sensory tentacles on the edge of the mouth. They are burrowing animals, spending much of their time in damp leaf litter, or in shallow fresh water. Some species have aquatic larval stages, others lay their eggs on land or give birth to live young. All are predatory, ambushing earthworms and other invertebrates. The most widespread and abundant caecilians in Seychelles are *Grandisonia alternans* and *Hypogeophis rostratus*. *G. alternans* is black, with the fore part of the head yellow-grey. It occurs under stones and in leaf litter from sea level to 750m, on all the four large granitic islands and Frégate. It reaches 33cm long. Four other members of the genus *Grandisonia* are all smaller than this species. *Hypogeophis rostratus* has been recorded from Mahé, Praslin, Silhouette, La Digue, Curieuse, Ste Anne, Frégate and Cerf. Unlike some caecilians, it does not require water for breeding or the development of young; the eggs are laid in clutches in moist terrestrial sites, and the female remains coiled around them until they hatch. The adults occur in leaf litter, under stones and in marshes, and reach a length of 20cm.

Sooglossid Frogs

The family Sooglossidae is endemic to the Seychelles, with four species in two genera (*Sooglossus* and *Nesomantis*), restricted to the uplands of Mahé and Silhouette. All are small, and one is among the smallest frogs in the world. They are mainly nocturnal in their activity. Unlike most frogs, they do not require water bodies in which to breed; all lay their eggs on the ground. In some species, the tadpole is carried on the back of the adult, while in others the tadpole stage takes place entirely within the egg, the young animal hatching as a fully developed froglet. The commonest and most widespread of the sooglossids is the pygmy frog *Sooglossus gardineri*, which can be found as low as 200m above sea level, especially in the wetter North-west Monsoon period. The other species are more restricted to higher altitudes.

Seychelles Pygmy Frog   *Sooglossus gardineri*

Grenuiy Nen | Length (snout-vent) 1.2cm | Endemic
Found: granitics; Mahé, Silhouette

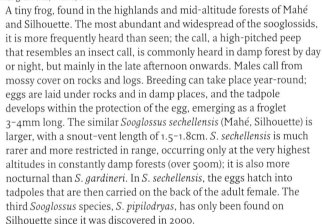

A tiny frog, found in the highlands and mid-altitude forests of Mahé and Silhouette. The most abundant and widespread of the sooglossids, it is more frequently heard than seen; the call, a high-pitched peep that resembles an insect call, is commonly heard in damp forest by day or night, but mainly in the late afternoon onwards. Males call from mossy cover on rocks and logs. Breeding can take place year-round; eggs are laid under rocks and in damp places, and the tadpole develops within the protection of the egg, emerging as a froglet 3–4mm long. The similar *Sooglossus sechellensis* (Mahé, Silhouette) is larger, with a snout–vent length of 1.5–1.8cm. *S. sechellensis* is much rarer and more restricted in range, occurring only at the very highest altitudes in constantly damp forests (over 500m); it is also more nocturnal than *S. gardineri*. In *S. sechellensis*, the eggs hatch into tadpoles that are then carried on the back of the adult female. The third *Sooglossus* species, *S. pipilodryas*, has only been found on Silhouette since it was discovered in 2000.

Nesomantis thomasseti

Grenuiy Nen | Length (snout-vent) 3.5–4.5cm | Endemic
Found: granitics; Mahé, Silhouette

The largest of the four species of sooglossid frog endemic to Seychelles – the other three all belong to the genus *Sooglossus* (*see* below). *Nesomantis* is predominantly brown in colour. It is restricted to high-altitude moist forests on Mahé and Silhouette (over about 400m), where it is active at night. Little is known about its reproductive behaviour or ecology.

Family Hyperoliidae – Reed and Sedge Frogs

The Hyperoliidae is a widespread African family of large tree frogs, with one representative in Seychelles.

Seychelles Tree Frog   *Tachycnemis seychellensis (Megalixus seychellensis)*

Krapo | Length to 4cm | Endemic
Found: granitics; Mahé, Praslin, Silhouette, La Digue

A large tree frog found on Mahé, Praslin, Silhouette and La Digue, from the coastal plateau (on La Digue) to high altitudes; perhaps most abundant in mid-altitude forests. The males (*a*) are usually red-brown in colour and the females (*b*) are larger and green. The species is nocturnal, and by day individuals rest on tree leaves (*c*), becoming pale and waxy in colour. Unlike the sooglossids, the tree frog has an aquatic tadpole stage. Adults are active by night, the males calling from vegetation and rocks around suitable water bodies such as pools and streams, especially during the peak breeding season around December. Eggs are laid on vegetation above the water and, on hatching, the young tadpoles fall into the water where they develop until metamorphosis.

Family Ranidae – True Frogs

The Ranidae is a huge family of typical frogs, with representatives all around the world. In Seychelles, there is one widespread, and possibly introduced, species.

Mascarene Frog   *Ptychadaena mascareniensis (Rana mascareniensis)*

Grenuiy | Length to 7cm | ?Introduced
Found: granitics (most islands)

The only non-endemic amphibian of Seychelles, this is a widespread frog found across a large part of Africa, from Egypt to Madagascar. It is a typical terrestrial frog in appearance, with pointed snout and long legs. Large females may reach 7cm long, although most individuals are considerably smaller. Adults are active by day and night, the males calling from puddles and ponds where the frogs gather to breed. The eggs hatch into aquatic tadpoles. The species is found from the coastal plateau to 450m or more, in a range of habitats including open areas, coconut plantations and gardens; it is the most common frog around human habitation. Found on many islands in the granitic group.

Fish

The fish fauna of Seychelles includes a small number of species in freshwater habitats (only on the granitic islands), rather higher species diversity in brackish streams, mangrove and other coastal habitats, and a rich and diverse marine fauna, especially around coral reefs. While only a handful of species occur in fresh water, the marine environment has at least 900 species.

Freshwater habitats in Seychelles are restricted in extent and are rather species-poor, and until recently only one truly freshwater fish native to Seychelles was known to science, a killifish. Several other fish enter fresh water from the sea, with one, the eel, spending a considerable part of its lifecycle in freshwater habitats. However, the most prominent fish in fresh water is an introduced species, the Tilapia. The keeping of exotic freshwater aquarium fish has recently become a widespread hobby, so it is likely that some of these species will establish in natural habitats in years to come. Freshwater habitats and species are absent from most of the coralline islands.

Mangroves and estuaries have their own distinct fauna, as well as providing a 'nursery' for juveniles of many marine fishes. Perhaps the most interesting residents of mangrove habitats are the mudskippers; their many adaptations to life on land enable them to exploit a range of microhabitats in the productive mangrove system. Rockskippers have a similar amphibious lifestyle in the splash zone on rocky coasts.

There is a huge diversity of marine fish in Seychelles, and it cannot be covered adequately in this book. Here, we have concentrated on a range of species that occur in shallow water environments, particularly coral reefs. Most of these species should be easily seen when snorkelling. Divers and keen snorkellers will find it necessary to obtain a book giving a more complete treatment of the marine fish fauna (e.g. Lieske and Myers, 1994). Although corals around the granitic islands have been devastated by periods of high water temperature caused by El Niño events in recent years, many of the colourful fish associated with the reef survive.

Most of the fish species of Seychelles are widespread in the Indo-Pacific region, although there are a few endemics. The marine fish fauna of the northernmost islands is therefore similar to that of Aldabra, although there are a few variations; for example, the colourful anthias *Pseudanthias squamipinnis* occurs at Aldabra but is not seen around the granitics and some of the larger food fish are less common around the granitic islands, where they are exploited, than at Aldabra.

OPPOSITE: Manta Ray (*Manta birostris*) with symbiotic remora fish.

Freshwater Fish

Tilapia *Oreochromis mossambicus* (*Tilapia mossambica*)
Tilaphya or Tilapya | Length to 39cm | Introduced

Large shoals of this fish can be seen in streams and mangrove areas of granitic islands. Adult males have the potential to reach 39cm long but are rarely this large in Seychelles. They dig small pits in muddy or sandy substrate, where breeding takes place; after laying the eggs, the female broods the eggs and small fry in her mouth for protection. It is omnivorous, eating fish as well as algae and insects. Although introduced as a food fish, it is rarely eaten in Seychelles.

Seychelles Killifish or Golden Panchax *Pachypanchax playfairii*
Gourzon | Length to 10cm | ?Endemic
Found: granitics; Mahé, Praslin, Silhouette

A small fish, up to 10cm in length but usually much less, found in brackish or freshwater habitats from mangrove to high-altitude streams on Mahé, Praslin and Silhouette. Juveniles are straw-coloured, while adults have brilliant reflective green and red spots. In males, these spots extend onto the fins. Females are less brightly coloured, with a black spot at the base of the dorsal fin. Killifish feed on insects, worms and crustaceans. In some lowland streams, the similar-looking introduced guppy *Poecilia reticulata* (called *Milyon* in Creole) occurs. Male guppies usually have colourful fins and the drab females have a rounded belly.

Eel *Anguilla bicolor*
Ange | Length 1m+ | Native

A large, yellow-brown eel. Adults may reach 1m or more long and are very thick-bodied. They may be found at all altitudes and can travel overland for short distances. Found on Mahé, Praslin, Silhouette, La Digue, Curieuse and probably smaller islands, as well as Aldabra. Like other *Anguilla* species, adults return to the sea to breed – the breeding site is unknown.

Fish of Mangroves and Rocky Coasts

Mudskippers and rockskippers, though belonging to different fish families, both lead an amphibious lifestyle in their habitats.

Common Mudskipper *Periophthalmus kalolo*

Kabo Soter | Length to 14cm | Native

There are two species of mudskipper in Seychelles: *P. argentilineatus* and *P. kalolo*. Both are extraordinary amphibious fish, mainly found in mangrove habitats. They spend most of their time out of water, clambering over roots and mud to feed on small invertebrates. Life on land, even in a damp and humid habitat like the mud banks of a mangrove forest, is difficult for a fish, and these species show several unusual adaptations to their environment. They use their pectoral fins for locomotion and the cheek pouches fill with water, allowing the gills to function normally while the fish is on land, although most of the fish's oxygen while it is out of the water comes through the damp skin. The eyes of the mudskipper are situated on top of the head for all-round vision, and to permit the animal to see out of water.

Rockskipper *Alticus anjouanae* (*Damania anjouanae*)

Kabo Marar | Length to 8cm | Native

At least 21 species of rockskipper (in the blenny family) occur in Seychelles, many of which live in rock pools or on exposed rocks in the splash zone of rocky coasts. *Alticus anjouanae* is one of the smaller species, reaching only 8cm. Males have a small crest (absent in females), and a dorsal fin with pronounced rays. They live on and around rocks in the littoral zone, spending much of the time out of water, and feed on invertebrates in algal turf.

Marine Fish

Sharks and Rays

Sharks and rays are cartilaginous fish, lacking true bone in their skeleton. All are carnivorous, although shark attacks are very rare in Seychelles. Potentially dangerous species that regularly occur here include Blacktip Reef Shark, Tiger, Mako and Bull Sharks. Sharks are becoming rarer in many areas due to over-fishing for their fins. Several species of stingrays have the potential to inflict painful wounds.

FAMILY CARCHARHINIDAE – REQUIEM SHARKS

Blacktip Reef Shark *Carcharinus melanopterus*
Rekin Nwanr | Length to 1.8m

A common shark with black tips on all fins. Small individuals are seen in shallows close to shore, and in lagoons. Adults are more common around outer coral reefs and have been known to attack humans.

FAMILY RHINCODONTIDAE – WHALE SHARK

Whale Shark *Rhincodon typus*
Sagren | Length to 12m+

The dorsal surface of this shark is blue-grey, with numerous pale spots. It feeds on plankton and smaller fish, often swimming close to the water surface. It is a migratory species of tropical oceans, but there may be a semi-resident population in Seychelles' waters. Around Mahé, there seem to be two peaks in sightings: June–August and October–December. Some of the fish here have been tagged, with numbered tags inserted close to the dorsal fin; if one is seen, the number and details should be recorded and reported to the Marine Conservation Society of Seychelles.

FAMILY MYLIOBATIDAE – EAGLE RAYS

Spotted Eagle Ray *Aetobatus narinari*
Lare Sousouri | Width to 3.5m (usually much less)

Common in coastal waters of the Seychelles, where it feeds on molluscs and crustaceans. Seen singly or in groups, sometimes in large shoals, over reefs, sandy shores or seagrass beds.

FAMILY DASYATIDAE – STINGRAYS

Feathertail Stingray *Pastinachus sephen*
Lare Plim | Length to 3m

A yellow-brown stingray with a grey fleshy lobe on the tail. It occurs in shallow lagoons and around coral reefs, often part-covered in sand. The tail spines can give a painful and dangerous sting.

Reef Fish

Coral reefs are the main centre of fish biodiversity in Seychelles, and a selection of species is described here.

FAMILY MURAENIDAE – MORAY EELS A family of large, eel-like predators with sharp-toothed jaws. Many species lurk in reef caves during the day, with only their gaping mouth visible.

Snowflake Moray Eel *Echidna nebulosa*

Kong | Length to 80cm

This brightly patterned species inhabits crevices in the reef and is mainly active at night. Young individuals are found in shallow water, under rocks. It feeds on crustaceans and fish. Also shown is the Peppered Moray *Siderea picta*, a larger species to 1.2m.

FAMILY HEMIRAMPHIDAE – HALFBEAKS Long-bodied, surface-dwelling fish with an elongate process on the lower jaw.

Spotted Halfbeak *Hemiramphus far*

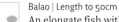

Balao | Length to 50cm

An elongate fish with four dark spots on each side of the silvery body, and a long 'beak'. The upper lobe of the tail is yellow and the lower lobe blue. Often seen in groups, feeding close to the surface.

FAMILY HOLOCENTRIDAE – SOLDIERFISH AND SQUIRRELFISH Medium-sized fish, many nocturnal, with large eyes. Often red, or with red-and-white stripes.

Red Soldierfish *Myripristis murdjan*

Lyon Gro Lizve | Length to 27cm

A shoaling, mainly nocturnal fish species, seen by day lurking under overhanging rocks or in dark, sheltered parts of the reef. It can be identified by the black band through its eyes and a black mark on the gill cover.

Seychelles Squirrelfish *Sargocentron seychellense*

Lyon | Length to 25cm

A common shallow-water reef species, often active by day. Occurs in groups around corals and off rocky shores.

FAMILY AULOSTOMIDAE – TRUMPETFISH Long-bodied lurking predators. Only one species occurs in Seychelles' waters.

Trumpetfish *Aulostomus chinensis*

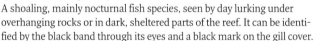

Tronpet | Length to 80cm

A common predator that occurs in two colour phases, one brown-grey (pictured), the other bright yellow. It waits, inactive, to ambush smaller fish.

FAMILY SYNGNATHIDAE – PIPEFISH AND SEAHORSES A family of slow-moving, long-bodied fish. There are few seahorses in the Seychelles but at least six species of pipefish occur.

Trachyramphus bicoarctatus
Length to 30cm

An elongate, slow-moving fish lacking a caudal fin. Found among reefs and seagrasses in coastal shallows. The mouth is at the tip of a long tubular snout.

FAMILY SCORPAENIDAE – SCORPIONFISH A family of medium-sized fishes with very venomous fin spines, including the highly camouflaged stonefish *Synanceia verrucosa*, the world's most venomous fish.

Indian Lionfish *Pterois miles*
Pwason Arme | Length to 40cm

A beautiful but well-camouflaged fish, with long-spined pectoral and dorsal fins. These fins have venomous spines that can give a very painful sting. This is a large-mouthed ambushing predator, feeding on smaller fish.

FAMILY SERRANIDAE – GROUPERS AND ANTHIASES The groupers include some very large fish, many of them important food fish. The anthiases are small, very colourful shoaling fish. Twelve species have been recorded in Seychelles, but none occur around the granitic islands.

Foursaddle Grouper *Epinephelus spilotoceps*
Vyey Sat | Length to 31cm

Epinephelus is a large genus with about 21 species in Seychelles' waters, from around 30cm in length to 2m. Several smaller, attractively patterned species such as this one inhabit reefs. One of the largest species in Seychelles' waters is the Potato Cod *Epinephelus tukula*; adults (up to 2m in length) inhabit caves at depths of 20m or more. All groupers are predators of fish and invertebrates.

FAMILY CIRRHITIDAE – HAWKFISHES A family of small grouper-like predatory fish. Only three species are known in Seychelles.

Freckled Hawkfish *Paracirrhites forsteri*
Length to 22cm

The Freckled Hawkfish is commonly seen perching among corals during the day. It feeds on small fishes and shrimps. Males maintain a harem of females within a territory.

FAMILY CARANGIDAE – JACKS AND TREVALLYS A family of medium-large silvery fishes, including many active, shoaling species and food fish.

Silver Pompano   *Trachinotus blochii*

Pompe, Lune | Length to 110cm

Trachinotus species have laterally flattened bodies with a distinctive oval silhouette. This species has yellowish fins, and is commonly seen in groups. Juveniles occur in very shallow areas close to shore, while adults are more frequent in deeper waters off seaward reefs.

FAMILY NEMIPTERIDAE – THREADFIN BREAM A small family of elongate, small fishes with rather forked tails.

Bridled Threadfin Bream or Bridled Spinecheek   *Scolopsis frenatus*

Ivano, Zano | Length to 26cm

A common carnivore of benthic invertebrates, found over shallow reefs to depths of around 20m. Juveniles occur in small groups or alone in shallower waters. As they grow older, the colours become duller and adults tend to form larger groups.

FAMILY LETHRINIDAE – EMPERORS A family of medium-large snapper-like fishes, usually with a large mouth and forked tail.

Blackspot, or Thumbprint, Emperor   *Lethrinus harak*

Anba Lasann | Length to 60cm

A common fish species of shallow waters, especially over sandy or muddy substrates, for example off sandy beaches, in mangroves, seagrass beds and lagoons. Feeds on benthic invertebrates.

FAMILY MULLIDAE – GOATFISHES Elongate fishes with a pair of long barbels beneath the chin, which they use to detect prey on the seabed, in sandy or muddy substrates.

Longbarbel Goatfish   *Parupeneus macronema*

Rouze | Length to 30cm

A common goatfish, recognised by its red-purple coloration and the dark base of the second dorsal fin. It forages over sandy substrates on reef flats by day, from shallows to a depth of around 25m.

FAMILY HAEMULIDAE – SWEETLIPS AND GRUNTS A family of large, generally nocturnal fishes, similar to snappers.

Oriental Sweetlips   *Plectorhinchus vittatus*

Kaka Matlo | Length to 45cm

Adults (pictured) occur alone or in small schools on reefs. Juveniles have very different markings – they are chocolate brown with cream blotches – and are rather shy, hiding among coral. Both adult and young feed on benthic invertebrates.

FAMILY EPHIPPIDAE – BATFISH OR SPADEFISHES Juvenile Batfish have elongate fins, and occur in mangroves or shallow coastal waters. The adults are rounded and become very large. They are omnivorous, eating algae and small invertebrates.

Longfin Batfish *Platax teira*
Pouldo | Length to 50cm

Juveniles have very elongate dorsal and ventral fins, and distinct dark brown stripes. The similar Circular Batfish *P. orbicularis* is distinguished when adult by the lack of the dark spot at the front of the anal fin. Batfish often occur in shoals and are not shy of humans.

FAMILY CHAETODONTIDAE – BUTTERFLYFISH The butterflyfishes are small, laterally flattened, disc-shaped, brightly coloured reef fish. Most feed on coral polyps or algae. There are at least 21 species in Seychelles' waters, all called Papiyon in Creole.

Threadfin Butterflyfish *Chaetodon auriga*
Papiyon | Length to 20cm

A common butterflyfish, with the posterior rays of the dorsal fin elongated into a threadlike process. Feeds on corals, anemones and other invertebrates, and algae.

Halfmoon, or Racoon, Butterflyfish *Chaetodon lunula*
Papiyon | Length to 20cm

Young fish often occur in shallow water among coastal rocks, while adults inhabit reefs. They feed by night as well as during the day on a wide range of invertebrates including coral polyps, and algae.

Black-backed Butterflyfish *Chaetodon melannotus*
Papiyon | Length to 15cm

A species of lagoons, reef flats and less-exposed seaward reefs, where it is usually seen in pairs.

Meyer's Butterflyfish *Chaetodon meyeri*
Papiyon | Length to 19cm

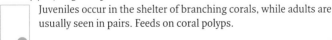
Juveniles occur in the shelter of branching corals, while adults are usually seen in pairs. Feeds on coral polyps.

Purple, Rip or Redfin Butterflyfish *Chaetodon trifasciatus*
Papiyon | Length to 15cm

The fins of the adult may show some purple, although none of the English names of this butterflyfish seem particularly appropriate. Adults are usually seen in pairs and feed on coral polyps.

Zanzibar Butterflyfish *Chaetodon zanzibariensis*
Papiyon | Length to 12cm

An attractive species of lagoons and seaward reefs, to a depth of 30m. Adults are usually seen alone or in pairs, and feed on coral polyps.

FAMILY POMACANTHIDAE – ANGELFISH Angelfish are medium-sized, colourful reef fishes. Males defend both a territory and a harem of females. Juveniles often differ significantly from adults in colour and pattern.

Three-spot Angelfish *Apolemicthys trimaculatus*
Length to 25cm

A relatively small angelfish that occurs in lagoons and seaward reefs to depths of 40m and feeds mainly on sponges and tunicates.

Emperor Angelfish *Pomacanthus imperator*
Length to 40cm

The large, attractively marked adults are seen in deeper parts of reefs, and feed mostly on sponges. The juveniles are very different in appearance; they are predominantly blue with a pattern of concentric circular white lines. Juveniles are frequently seen in shallower parts of reefs.

Semicircle, or Koran, Angelfish *Pomacanthus semicirculatus*
Length to 40cm

A commonly seen solitary angelfish. Juveniles are similar in colour to those of *P. imperator*, but the white lines do not form complete circles. At 10cm or more, the fish transforms into the adult pattern, which is predominantly dull blue-grey with a bright blue edge to body and fins. Feeds on sponges, tunicates and algae.

FAMILY POMACENTRIDAE – DAMSELFISH A family of small, often colourful, reef fish. Some are shoaling plankton-feeders and omnivores, others are territorial and aggressive, defending patches of rock on which algal turf grows. Anemonefish live in association with sea anemones, immune to their stings.

Sergeant Major or Indo-Pacific Sergeant *Abudefduf vaigiensis*

Bweter | Length to 17cm
A small shoaling fish of coastal waters, often high in the water column. Huge groups can form where they are regularly fed by snorkellers.

Zebra Humbug or Humbug Dascyllus *Dascyllus aruanus*

Length to 10cm
A distinctively marked damselfish frequently seen in small shoals around branching coral heads on reefs.

Skunk Anemonefish or Clownfish *Amphiprion akallopisos*

Length to 10cm

Anemonefish are damselfish that live in close association with anemones, finding protection in the anemone's stinging tentacles, and are themselves protected from the stings of the anemone's tentacles by a coating of mucus. Anemonefishes all mature as males, but some change sex later, depending on their environment. A large mature female dominates the colony.

FAMILY LABRIDAE – WRASSES A large family, with about 60 species in Seychelles. Many show sexual dimorphism and their colours and patterns also differ with age, making identification difficult. In many wrasse, female fish have the capacity to change sex, depending on environmental conditions (e.g. competition from other males). Most are carnivorous, and some species are specialist 'cleaners', picking pests and mucus from larger fish.

Barred Thicklip, or 5-Banded, Wrasse *Hemigymnus fasciatus*

Mamzel Adele, Tamarin | Length to 50cm
Juveniles of this wrasse are brown with narrow yellow vertical stripes. Adults develop this distinctive banded black and white pattern. Feeds on a variety of benthic invertebrates among rocks and corals.

Hardwicke's, or Sixbar, Wrasse *Thalassoma hardwickei*

Kakatwa Lezar | Length to 18cm

A solitary wrasse species of shallow water, to around 15m deep, feeding on small crustaceans and fish. The attractive pattern varies little with age and sex, although males are slightly brighter. Found throughout Seychelles.

Goldbar Wrasse *Thalassoma hebraicum*
Kakatwa Lezar | Length to 23cm

A common wrasse, easily identified when adult by the golden yellow bar just behind the head. The juveniles are black with yellow spots. It is found in lagoons and reefs to 30m deep throughout Seychelles.

FAMILY SCARIDAE – PARROTFISHES Like wrasse, parrotfish display bright colours that vary with age and sex. All have a horny 'beak' used to feed on corals and to scrape algae from rocks. The powdered remains of coral in their excrement form part of the white sandy beaches of the tropics. Parrotfish are diurnal; by night they sleep in crevices in rocks and reefs, surrounded by a protective coat of mucus.

Bullethead Parrotfish *Chlorurus sordidus* (*Scarus sordidus*)
Kakatwa | Length to 40cm

Juveniles often occur in groups in lagoons and around shallow reefs; they are dark reddish brown, usually with some white spots on the flanks and a white blotch bearing a black spot at the base of the tail. Adult males (as shown here) are largely solitary reef-dwellers. A very widespread and variable parrotfish, found throughout the Indian and Pacific Oceans.

FAMILY SPHYRAENIDAE – BARRACUDAS A family of large, active predators, all with an elongate, laterally flattened shape. They are said to sometimes attack humans carrying shiny objects such as diving knives.

Great Barracuda *Sphyraena barracuda*
Bekin | Length to 190cm

Juveniles of this large predator occur in shallow waters close to shore, while solitary adults may occur in a range of habitats from the shallows of lagoons to the deep water of seaward reefs and the open ocean. Found throughout Seychelles. Although equipped with sharp teeth, they do not attack swimmers under normal circumstances.

FAMILY ZANCLIDAE – MOORISH IDOL The Moorish Idol is a relative of the surgeonfishes but lacks the tail spines typical of that family. There is only one, distinctive species.

Moorish Idol *Zanclus cornatus*
Tranchwa | Length to 25cm

The Moorish Idol is a beautiful fish with a distinctive silhouette. The elongate tubular snout is used to feed on sponges. They usually occur singly or in small groups, but are occasionally seen in large shoals. Found throughout Seychelles.

FAMILY ACANTHURIDAE – SURGEONFISHES AND UNICORNFISHES

Surgeonfish have a pair of sharp, retractable blades at the base of the tail. They are mostly medium-sized, laterally flattened reef fish. Unicornfish are generally larger, and some species have a pronounced 'horn' on the forehead.

Powder Blue Surgeon   *Acanthurus leucosternon*

Sirizyen | Length to 25cm

An instantly recognisable species, only likely to be confused with the Royal Tang (or Blue Tang) *A. hepatus*, which is a darker blue with a black stripe from eye to tail, dark blue dorsal fin tipped black, and yellow caudal fin with black marginal stripes. Powder Blue Surgeons are often seen in pairs or in large groups in shallow water over reefs, and feed on filamentous algae. Found throughout Seychelles.

Blue-lined, or Striped, Surgeonfish   *Acanthurus lineatus*

Sirizyen | Length to 38cm

A common surgeonfish, usually seen alone as adults because males are territorial and aggressive, protecting an area of algal turf where they feed. Young fish may be seen in small groups. Found throughout Seychelles.

Sailfin Tang   *Zebrasoma desjardinii*

Tabak | Length to 40cm

A less common species, occurring alone or in pairs, over reefs and in lagoons. Juveniles, with fins longer in proportion to the body, favour shallow, sheltered areas. Found throughout Seychelles.

Yellowkeel, or Orangespine, Unicornfish   *Naso lituratus*

Length to 50cm

A common unicornfish in Seychelles' waters, which lacks a horn but can be recognised by the yellow-orange area at the front of the head, running up from the eye to the yellow dorsal fin. It occurs in inshore areas, reefs and lagoons and feeds on algae. Found throughout Seychelles.

FAMILY SIGANIDAE – RABBITFISHES   The rabbitfish have venomous spines in the dorsal, anal and pelvic fins (can be very painful but not dangerous). Most species feed on algae, and they are a favoured food fish in Seychelles.

Blackeye Rabbitfish   *Siganus corallinus*

Kordonyen Lafimen, Kordonyen Brizan | Length to 30cm

Juveniles often occur in small groups in seagrass beds and lagoons; adults are found in pairs or small groups around reefs. They feed on algae and sponges. A popular food fish in Seychelles.

FAMILY BALISTIDAE – TRIGGERFISHES Triggerfish are generally solitary and aggressive. They have a characteristic shape, with the eyes set very high on the body. The mouth has heavy teeth, and the first dorsal fin has a large spine.

Picasso Trigger *Rhinecanthus aculeatus*

Bours | Length to 28cm

The Picasso Trigger has unmistakeable markings. It is usually seen singly or in pairs or, sometimes, small groups, often in shallow sandy areas on the landward side of reefs. It feeds on benthic invertebrates and algae.

FAMILY OSTRACIIDAE – TRUNKFISHES OR BOXFISHES Boxfishes have an exoskeleton of bony plates, and many have angular shapes. As a result, their movement is restricted and they are rather slow swimmers.

Spotted Trunkfish *Ostracion meleagris*

Kof | Length to 16cm

The male of this species is brightly coloured as in the photo, while the female is brown with cream spots. Feeds on invertebrates.

FAMILY TETRAODONTIDAE – PUFFERFISH A family of small to medium-sized fish, most of which have tough (but flexible) skin. Many species have toxic skin or internal organs, offering protection from predators.

Black-saddled Toby *Canthigaster valentini*

Length to 10cm

This small, brightly coloured pufferfish is protected from predators by toxins in its skin. The harmless filefish *Paraleuteres prionurus* mimics it, with very similar markings. It is a territorial species: males defend a territory and a harem of females.

FAMILY DIODONTIDAE – PORCUPINEFISH Porcupinefish have prominent spines all over the body and are capable of inflating with water when threatened, forming a ball-like mass of spines. They have large eyes and a powerful beak to crush hard-shelled invertebrates.

Common Porcupinefish *Diodon hystrix*

Bours Arme | Length to 80cm

This is a circumtropical species, found in the Indo-Pacific, Caribbean and Atlantic. Juveniles are pelagic, with adults settling on shallow reefs, where they are largely nocturnal, skulking in protected places during the day. Feeds on hard-shelled invertebrates.

Marine Invertebrates

Invertebrate animals are most prominent in marine habitats such as the reef, which indeed would not exist without reef-building hard corals, made up of many small individual animals (polyps). However, there are also many hidden species, especially those buried in sediments. Many are active at night and are rarely seen during the day, when they seek shelter and protection under sand or in rocky caves.

Molluscs
Marine molluscs include the familiar seashells, as well as chitons, sea slugs and cephalopods (octopus and squid). The shell-bearing molluscs include the snail-like gastropods and the bivalves such as mussels and clams, with paired, hinged shells. Some of the gastropods found in Seychelles' waters are highly decorative, including the cowries, cone shells and conches. However, all the specimens offered for sale in shops have been collected as live animals from the reefs – either here, or elsewhere in the region. Some, such as the Giant Triton, are endangered by such collection. Please do not buy shells. Even collecting empty shells from the beach should be done with care. Most empty shells (except cowries) are potential homes for hermit crabs – never collect a shell with a resident crab. The white sand of Seychelles is composed of pieces of ground-down shell and coral, so the shells should be left to ensure a future supply of sand.

Many of the molluscs found in Seychelles have planktonic larvae, allowing them a wide distribution within the region and beyond.

Class Polyplacophora (Chitons)

FAMILY CHITONIDAE
Several species of chiton occur in Seychelles and are difficult to differentiate, although all are easily recognised as chitons by their elongate shape and plated appearance. They are found on rocks (like limpets) just below the water surface. The photo shows *Acanthopleura* sp. (Chiton, Lalang Melani).

OPPOSITE: *Phyllidia varicosa.*

Class Gastropoda (Snails and Sea Slugs)

Most gastropods are snail-like animals, with a shell into which the body can retreat when danger threatens. Some gastropod species have a 'door' which seals the aperture of the shell, called the operculum. The sea slugs, although included in the Gastropoda, generally have reduced shells, or no shell at all.

FAMILY TROCHIDAE – TOP SHELLS A family of sea snails with pointed, conical shells, usually with a flattened base. The shells are either black and white or pink-red in colour. Most species graze on algae, although some eat sponges. At least ten species occur in Seychelles.

Red Top Shell *Trochus maculates*
Height to 7cm

A large, common and distinctive top shell up to 7cm tall, with pink-red markings. The underside has an umbilicus and the inner edge of the aperture, the columella, has a row of nodules or teeth. The similar but slightly smaller species *T. virgatus* has a shell whose height usually exceeds the width, lacks an umbilicus and lacks teeth on the columella.

FAMILY TURBINIDAE – TURBAN SHELLS Turbans are large, heavy shells. The living snails have a heavy, domed operculum that is used to seal the shell against predators. The empty shells are much used by land hermit crabs. There are around five species in Seychelles.

Green Snail *Turbo marmoratus*
Birgo | Height to 20cm

A huge snail, much collected in the past for mother-of-pearl. Shells with outer layers stripped away to reveal the glossy mother-of-pearl are often sold at tourist shops. This is the largest turban shell in Seychelles. It occurs below the low water mark in reef and rock crevices, off granitic and coralline islands. The similar, smaller, *T. setosus* is more common.

FAMILY NERITIDAE – NERITES A family of heavy, rounded or elongate shells, which fill a similar niche to limpets, feeding on microscopic algae in the littoral zone by night. Around nine species occur in Seychelles.

Nerita plicata
Bigarno | Length to 3cm

A small, pink or yellowish globular species with pronounced teeth on the inner lip of the aperture. Occurs on rocks in the upper littoral zone and above the high water mark.

Nerita textilis
Bigorno | Length to 5cm

A nerite with a more oblong shape than *N. plicata*, and a heavily sculptured outer surface. The shell has distinctive black and white markings. A common nerite above the high water mark.

FAMILY LITTORINIDAE – PERIWINKLES Small molluscs, shells with pointed spires, found in the littoral zone. At least five species in Seychelles.

Nodilittorina millegrana

Ti Mari | Height to 1.5cm

A small, rounded periwinkle, found clustered on rocks in the upper littoral zone and above the high water mark, often alongside nerites.

FAMILY JANTHINIDAE – VIOLET SHELLS A family of molluscs with distinctive violet-coloured fragile shells.

Violet Sea Snail *Janthina janthina*

Height 3cm

The shell of this species is thin and fairly fragile, resembling the shell of a land snail. A pantropical planktonic species, carried on its mucus bubbles, which are occasionally still attached to stranded specimens.

FAMILY POTAMIDIDAE – MUD WHELKS A family of heavy, tall-spired shells. In life, the animals possess a thin operculum. The animals feed on algae, often in mangrove habitats. One species is found in Seychelles.

Mud Creeper *Terebralia palustris*

Fizo | Height to 15cm

A large spired shell, common in mangrove swamps and tidal streams, where large groups can be seen grazing on the algal film on muddy substrates in shallow water. The empty shells are often used by Mangrove Hermit Crabs.

FAMILY STROMBIDAE – CONCHES Conches are large molluscs with heavy, thick-walled and often very decorative shells.

Spider Conch *Lambis chiragra arthritica*

Kokiy Lapat | Length to 17cm

An attractive medium-sized conch. Young specimens (lower example in photograph) have no spines, but as animals mature, the spines lengthen. It occurs on sandy substrates in shallow areas. At least two other *Lambis* species occur in Seychelles, the Giant Spider Conch *L. truncata* (shell to 38cm) and *L. crocata*, to 17cm with seven marginal spines.

FAMILY CYPRAEIDAE – COWRIES (PISLAZ) The shells of cowries are rounded with an elongate narrow aperture with teeth on one or both sides. In the living animal, the fleshy mantle extends all over the outside of the shell. At least 46 species occur in Seychelles and the shells are often found on beaches, but the patterns are rapidly eroded by abrasion on sand. The illustration shows the following species: top row, left to right: Tortoise Cowrie *Cypraea testudinaria* (to 13cm), Tiger Cowrie *C. tigris*, Mole Cowrie *C. talpa*; bottom row, left to right: Money Cowrie *C. moneta*, *C. asellus*, Serpent's Head Cowrie *C. caputserpentis*, *C. histrio*.

FAMILY OVULIDAE – EGG COWRIES Closely related to the cowries, with glossy shells, usually pure white but obscured in life by the dark mantle.

Common Egg Cowrie *Ovula ovum*

Length to 12cm

This species has a porcelain-like white shell. In life, it is largely or entirely covered by the mantle, which is black with gold specks. It occurs on reefs at depths of 2m or more.

FAMILY MURICIDAE – ROCK SHELLS, MUREXES A large, varied family all with opercula. At least 48 species have been recorded in Seychelles.

Thais rudolphi

Height to 7cm

A medium-sized species with a relatively thick, dark, unspined shell. The interior is orange-pink towards the lip.

FAMILY BURSIDAE – FROG SHELLS A family of large, heavy shells.

Bursa bubo

Length to 20cm

This large heavy mollusc occurs on coral and rocky reefs. The exterior of the shell is roughly sculptured and often overgrown with encrusting animals and plants; the interior is shiny orange.

FAMILY FASCIOLARIIDAE – TULIP SHELLS A family of medium to large snails, the shells of which have a tall spire and elongate siphonal canal.

Pleuroploca filamentosa

Length to 15cm

A common tulip shell species with a narrow, whelk-like shell. The animal lives in shallow seagrass beds and reefs.

FAMILY BULLIDAE – THE BUBBLES Sea slugs with reduced fragile shells.

True Bubble *Bulla ampulla*

Length (shell) to 5cm, (extended body) to 10cm

The delicate glossy shell of this species may reach 5cm. The animal hides under sand by day, emerging at night to feed on algae.

FAMILY CONIDAE – CONE SHELLS (KON) The Conidae is a large family of carnivorous molluscs. They catch prey using dart-like modified teeth and toxins. The toxin of some species is potentially deadly to humans. In life, the shell is covered by a fibrous layer called the periostracum, which can completely obscure the shell's surface patterns. The photograph shows the following species: left, Geographer or Map Cone *Conus geographus* (to 15cm; potentially deadly); top right, *C. ebraeus*; bottom right, *C. chaldeus*.

FAMILY PHYLLIDIIDAE – PHYLLIDS A family of shell-less sea slugs. Some sequester toxins from their invertebrate prey and advertise their poisonous nature in bright colours.

Phyllidia varicosa

Length to 11cm

A colourful sea slug of coral reefs throughout the Indo-Pacific. Lacks a shell, but the bright skin colours indicate to predators that the animal is poisonous. A diurnal predator, feeding on sessile invertebrates on reefs.

Class Bivalvia – Bivalves

The bivalves have paired shells (valves), hinged on one side. Most are burrowers, moving through sediments with the aid of the large muscular foot. Some attach to rocks using a byssus. All are filter feeders.

FAMILY PINNIDAE – EAR SHELLS (LARSDAM) The photograph shows *Pinna muricata*, with a rather fragile, distinctively shaped shell to 15cm long. It is found in colonies in shallow seagrass beds and silty places where the shell is buried vertically in the substrate.

FAMILY TRIDACNIDAE – GIANT CLAMS Large bivalves of reefs. In life (*a*), the mantle is exposed at the edge of the gape; it may be green-brown or blue and contains symbiotic algae that supplement the food the clam obtains through filter feeding. Two *Tridacna* clams occur in Seychelles, *T. maxima*, with asymmetrical valves up to 30cm across (*b*) and *T. squamosa*, with a more symmetrically shaped shell to 35cm.

FAMILY DONACIDAE – BUTTERFLY, OR WEDGE, SHELLS A family of small-medium triangular bivalves, often brightly coloured, that live in sandy substrates. The photograph shows a *Donax* species called Tek Tek in Creole, found in sandy beaches, and traditionally gathered as a food. At least two species occur here, *D. cuneatus* and *D. faba*. Both are small (to 3cm long).

FAMILY PSAMMOBIIDAE A family of small-medium burrowing bivalves. The illustrated species, *Asaphis deflorata*, has a heavy shell to 8cm long and occurs in shallow water on sandy or silty sediments.

Class Cephalopoda – Cephalopods

The cephalopods are active molluscs with eight or more tentacle limbs. The class includes nautiluses, octopuses, squid and cuttlefishes.

Octopus vulgaris

Zourit | Length to 1m

Several species of octopus occur in shallow waters of the Seychelles, especially around reefs; when alive, they can change colour to match the substrate over which they pass. They are much hunted for food.

Crustacea

The phylum Crustacea includes crabs and lobsters, shrimps and barnacles. There are many species in Seychelles, most of them marine but including species found on beaches and in mangroves (in this section), as well as freshwater and terrestrial habitats (*see* 'Terrestrial Invertebrates' section).

Subclass Cirripedia – Barnacles

A group of sessile crustacea with planktonic larvae. Larvae settle out of the plankton onto suitable substrate. Barnacles form two basic groups: acorn barnacles and stalked (goose) barnacles. Acorn barnacles such as *Tetraclita squamosa* (*a*) occur on rocky shores; at low tide, they are protected by calcareous plates. When submerged in water, the modified legs project from the shell and are used for filter feeding. Goose barnacles *Lepas* spp. (*b*) grow on floating objects and ships, and may often be found on the beach attached to flotsam. Suitable surfaces are colonised very rapidly after becoming available. The body is encased in calcareous plates and attached to the substrate by a rubbery stalk.

Order Decapoda – Lobsters, Shrimps and Crabs

Cardisoma carnifex
Tyangoman | Width (carapace) to 10cm

A large land crab of both granitic and coralline islands; it is especially common in mangrove habitats – for example, on Curieuse Island – and on rocky inland areas of Aldabra. It builds burrows in muddy substrates. The carapace is red-purple, and slate-grey on the dorsal surface. Males develop enlarged claws, one larger than the other. When threatened, these claws are raised in defence, but the species is mainly vegetarian.

Ocypode ceratophthalma
Loulou Grangal | Width (carapace) to 4.5cm

This relatively large ghost crab is pale cream-grey with pronounced 'horns' above the eyes. It is found on sandy beaches throughout Seychelles. On less-disturbed islands, it is active during the day, but may be mainly crepuscular or nocturnal on busier beaches. When threatened, it retreats to the safety of its burrow, running rapidly across the sand. Ghost crabs are opportunist scavengers, feeding on living and dead plants and animals, including turtle eggs and young.

Ocypode cordimana
Loulou Grangal | Width (carapace) to 2.5cm

This is a smaller, stockier ghost crab, which lacks the 'horns' of *O. ceratophthalma*, and is usually blue-grey in colour rather than the pale yellow-grey of *O. ceratophthalma*. It is found on the upper beach, beach crest vegetation, grassy coastal areas and plateau woodland.

Fiddler Crabs: Genus *Uca* Fiddler crabs are found in mangrove habitats and similar places where muddy or silty substrates occur in the intertidal zone. In all species, females have two small front claws (chelae), used for feeding. These claws scoop up pieces of mud into the mouth, where it is sorted by the crab's mouthparts; tiny food particles are retained while sand and mud are expelled. In males, only one of the feeding claws is functional; the other has developed into a (relatively) huge signalling device. This large, colourful claw is used to communicate the male's ownership of territory and for courtship. Fiddler crabs rarely move far from their territory, and will rapidly retreat into the safety of their burrows when in danger. At least three species occur in Seychelles.

Uca lactea annulipes

Krab Semaphot | Width (carapace) to 1.5cm

The smallest and commonest fiddler crab in the granitic islands, with a pale grey-brown carapace. When observed closely, darker brown scribbled markings can be distinguished on the carapace. Most of the limbs are brown, but the enlarged foreclaw (chela) of the male is pale pink. This crab can occur in huge numbers on suitable mud- or sandbanks, often at the inland side of mangroves.

Uca chlorophthalmus

Krab Semaphot | Width (carapace) to 2cm

A larger, more impressive species with a jewel-like green-blue upper carapace. The limbs of this species are bright red basally, with pink chelae in males.

Mangrove Crab *Neosarmatium meinerti*

Loulou | Width (carapace) to 5cm

This common burrowing crab of mangrove habitats has bright scarlet chelae. It feeds on mangrove leaves that are dragged back to its burrow.

Sally-lightfoot Crab *Grapsus tenuicrustatus*

Karkasaye | Width (carapace) to 7cm

A flattened, agile and active crab of rocky shores that moves easily between sea and land and is usually seen clambering over rocks in the splash zone. While exposed to the air, they can move rapidly on steep and rugged surfaces and are not washed away by waves. A herbivore, feeding on algae in the littoral zone.

Echinoderms

The echinoderms include the sea urchins, sea cucumbers, starfish and relatives. The sea cucumbers are harvested and dried in large numbers in the region for export to the Far East where they are eaten.

Slate Pencil Urchin *Heterocentrotus* spp.

Latanye | Diameter (test) 10cm, Spines to 10cm

This urchin has heavy, thick spines, which may be red-brown or purplish.

Echinothrix diadema

Latanye | Diameter (test) to 20cm, Spines to 5cm

Several species of long-spined black sea urchins occur on shallow Seychelles' reefs. All graze on encrusting algae, and can remove the surface of coral rocks with their scraping mouthparts. The tips of the spines can break off in the skin causing severe pain.

Astropyga radiata

Latanye | Diameter (test) to 18cm, Spines to 5cm

The spines of this species are brown to orange with paler banding, and parts of the test are bare of spines and vivid orange-pink in colour.

Pearsonothuria graeffei (*Bohadschia graeffei*)

Bambara | Length to 50cm

A sea cucumber with warty grey-brown skin patterned with occasional narrow dark lines. The mouth is surrounded by 25 black tentacles, visible when the animal is feeding. It eats detritus and algae. A relatively common species, it can be seen on shallow reefs and sandy substrates.

Stichopus chloronotus

Bambara | Length to 30cm

A common sea cucumber in seagrass beds and shallow reef platforms. It is very dark green-black, square in cross section with raised conical tubercles at the angles.

Crown of Thorns Starfish *Acanthaster planci*

Zetwal Demer | Width to 60cm

This starfish feeds on corals, and outbreaks of this species have been blamed for extensive coral death in some places, although it appears rare in Seychelles. It reaches 60cm across, and has 16–30 arms.

Hydrozoans

Portuguese Man-o'-war *Physalia* spp.

Lagratel or Lagratel Parasol | Length to 1m

Generally species of the open ocean. Each is a colony of specialised individuals that cannot live apart. They are supported at the water surface by a gas-filled float. Large specimens can give a severe sting.

Corals

The corals are colonial invertebrates made up of polyps. In the soft corals, each polyp is embedded in a firm, leathery tissue. Soft corals rapidly colonise newly available substrates. Hard corals build a solid calcareous skeleton that forms the basis of the reef. In recent years all hard corals have been very badly hit by high sea temperatures. These conditions cause coral polyps to expel their symbiotic algal cells. Affected corals lose their colour (the process is called a bleaching event) and die. In 1998, up to 90 per cent of corals around the granitic islands were killed, and regenerating coral was again hit in 2002 and 2003. Reefs at the coralline islands and Aldabra were less severely affected. The identification of corals to species is very difficult in the field.

Leather Coral *Sarcophyton* spp.

Colony width to 1m

Leather corals are among the first to colonise reefs that have been affected by coral bleaching. With the polyps extended, they resemble large anemones. When the polyps are withdrawn, the surface looks smooth and leathery.

Blue Coral *Heliopora coerulea*

Koray Ble | Colony width to 1m

Although more closely related to soft corals, this species forms a hard calcium carbonate skeleton. The living polyps are pale grey-green, but the skeleton is a strong permanent blue colour. Pieces of blue coral are commonly found on beaches around the granitic islands.

Staghorn and Table Corals *Acropora* spp.

Colony width to 1m+ (depending on species)

Acropora is a large genus of branching corals. Some species are very fast-growing, the branches increasing in length by several centimetres per year, and these are important in exposed areas of reef. Staghorn coral *A. formosa* is a common bushy species, pale brown in colour with brightly coloured (pink, purple or blue) growing tips. Several *Acropora* species form tabular colonies, developing a tiered structure of plates.

Mushroom Coral *Fungia scutaria*

Koray Fler | Diameter to 18cm

Mushroom corals are unusual, solitary corals; large, individual polyps occur alone. The skeleton is circular or oval with prominent radial ribs, and cream-brown in colour. The polyp's tentacles are usually green.

Brain Coral *Platygyra* spp.

Colony width to 1m

A colonial coral forming a large domed structure with sinuous patterns of ridges on the surface. Several brain coral species exist in Seychelles' waters.

Land Invertebrates

Compared to that of the continental tropics, the land invertebrate fauna of Seychelles shows relatively limited species diversity, although a high proportion (perhaps 70 per cent) of the native species that do occur are endemic. Because of the unique geological history of the central islands, examples of some unlikely groups such as mayflies, caddis flies and land leeches survive. Endemic plant communities support endemic invertebrates; the damp, litter-filled leaf bases of endemic palms and *Pandanus* contain aerial communities of small endemic beetles and other insects, and one species of mosquito (*Urotaenia nepenthes*) passes its early aquatic stages in the 'pitchers' of pitcher plants. Even some of the smaller granitic islands support interesting endemic invertebrates, including the Frégate Island Giant Tenebrionid, a beetle endemic to Frégate island and apparently found nowhere else on earth.

On the low coralline islands, the proportion of endemic species is lower and invertebrate communities, like the habitats that support them, have been much influenced by human activities. Many species have been introduced, either unwittingly (as pests) or deliberately; for example, ladybirds were widely introduced to control scale insects on coconut crops.

The raised coralline islands of Aldabra have a narrower range of habitats than the granitic islands, and are a challenging environment to any invertebrates that require moist conditions. However, some groups such as dragonflies occur here and there is a range of colourful day-flying butterflies that are absent from the granitics. Around 40 per cent of the Aldabran insect fauna is endemic, but, unlike the endemic fauna of the granitics, which has strong links with Asia, that of Aldabra has mostly originated from Africa and Madagascar. Aldabra shares only about 4 per cent of its insect fauna with the granitic islands.

Molluscs – Land Snails

The land molluscs of Seychelles contain about 60 species of snail and several shell-less slugs. Many of these are endemic species and genera; on the granitic islands, the most diverse endemic genus is *Pachnodus*, which includes ten surviving species. Five *Pachnodus* species occur on Mahé, two on Praslin, three on Silhouette, one on Frégate, and evidence of extinct species has been found on La Digue and Curieuse. The largest and most obvious members of the snail fauna are the introduced Giant African Land Snails *Achatina* spp. Compared to the granitic islands, the fauna of the coralline islands is relatively small, but the Aldabra group supports a number of endemics.

OPPOSITE: Seychelles Milkweed Butterfly.

Stylodonta studeriana
Width to 7cm | Endemic
Found: granitics; Praslin

A large endemic snail, with a heavy yellow-brown shell, found in Coco de Mer palms in the Vallée de Mai and other palm forests on Praslin. A very similar species *S. unidentata* is found on Mahé and some satellite islands. Both are viviparous.

Pachnodus niger
Kolimason | Shell length to 2cm | Endemic
Found: granitics; Mahé, Praslin

A small snail, with a rather globular matt black shell, perhaps the most easily identified *Pachnodus* species. It is found on Mahé and Praslin in high- and mid-altitude forest (including palm forest). Like most *Pachnodus*, it is generally seen well above the ground on vegetation such as endemic palms. Other *Pachnodus* species, with more elongate shells, include *P. ornatus* (*b*), variable in colour but often pale brown with a darker ring on each whorl (mid–high altitudes on Mahé) and *P. fregatensis*, the only *Pachnodus* species on Frégate and an island endemic.

African Land Snail   *Achatina immaculata* (*A. panthera*)
Kourpa | Shell length to 27cm (rarely) | Introduced
Found: granitics | corallines

A huge land snail, originally from Africa but introduced throughout the tropics as a food source. *Achatina* species are rarely or never eaten here and they have become pests of crop plants. Two similar species occur in Seychelles: *A. immaculata* has a yellowish body, and the shell has a pink columella, while *A. fulica* has a greyish body. *Achatina* species include the largest terrestrial molluscs in the world: in *A. fulica* the shell may reach 27cm long, but individuals in Seychelles are always a lot smaller than this. The ecologically damaging carnivorous snails *Euglandina rosea* and *Gonaxis quadrilateralis* have been introduced in an effort to control *Achatina* species.

Vaginula seychellensis
Length 7cm (contracted), 15cm (extended) | Endemic
Found: granitics; Mahé, Praslin, Silhouette

Three related species of slug are native to the granitic Seychelles, and all have a flattened body with a marginal keel and blue-grey tentacles projecting from beneath. *V. seychellensis* is a large slug, and the most widespread and variable species, occurring on Mahé, Praslin and Silhouette, from sea level to high altitudes. A variety of colour forms occur, including mottled greyish, red-brown and white. In the Vallée de Mai, a white form of *V. seychellensis* feeds on the male flowers of the Coco de Mer.

Crustacea – Land Crabs

Land crabs play an important ecological role as scavengers, especially on remote coralline islands. All return to the sea to breed. The most terrestrial crabs are the land hermit crabs, with three common species in the granitic archipelago and a fourth large species largely restricted to the Aldabra group.

Geograpsus crinipes

Karkasay | Width (carapace) to 4.5cm | Native
Found: granitics | corallines | Aldabra
A medium-sized, long-legged land crab related to the Sally-lightfoot of rocky shores. Most commonly seen at dusk or in the early morning.

Coenobita brevimanus

Solda | Shield length to 2cm, uses shells to 15cm across | Native
Found: granitics | corallines | Aldabra

A large purple-brown land hermit crab, the largest species of the granitic islands. Like most other hermit crabs, it uses a seashell as protection for its soft abdomen. When disturbed, it retreats into the shell, sealing the aperture with the large claw. Larger specimens live in large turban shells or tulip shells, and occasionally the empty shells of coconuts.

Red Hermit Crab *Coenobita perlatus*

Solda | Shield length to 2cm, body c.8cm long | Native
Found: granitics | corallines | Aldabra
A medium-sized, bright red land hermit crab.

Coenobita rugosus

Solda | Shield length to 1cm, uses shells to 4cm across | Native
Found: granitics | corallines | Aldabra
A small, pale grey or beige land hermit crab, often seen climbing in vegetation.

Robber, or Coconut, Crab *Birgus latro*

Sipay, Krab Koko | Length to 60cm | Native
Found: Amirantes (St Joseph) | Aldabra

This widespread but threatened species, the largest land crab in the world, has been over-hunted for food in the granitic islands, Farquhar and elsewhere. Occasionally reported on the granitics, it is more abundant on some of the southern coralline islands. The Robber Crab may weigh up to 4kg. Its fearsome claws are used for tackling difficult foods such as coconuts, *Pandanus* fruits, young turtles and tortoises, and a variety of other plants and animals. It can climb small trees and Coconut Palms. Only very young robber crabs use mollusc shells for protection. Robber Crabs may be predominantly reddish in colour or blue-grey. They forage on land mainly at night, returning to the shelter of a burrow during the day.

Crustacea – Freshwater Species

Seychelles Freshwater Crab *Seychellum alluaudi*

Krab Larivyer or Krab Montangn | Width (carapace) to 4cm | Endemic
Found: granitics; Mahé, Praslin, Silhouette, La Digue

A freshwater crab of higher altitude streams in the granitic islands. This is an endemic species belonging to a group that is otherwise restricted to East Africa. The female carries her eggs attached to her abdomen and they hatch as small crabs. A second native species of freshwater crab, *Sesarmops impressum,* is found in streams at lower altitudes.

Crayfish *Macrobrachium* spp.

Kamaron or Kamaron Larivver | Length to 20cm | Native
Found: granitics; Mahé, Praslin, Silhouette, Curieuse

Crayfish are actually large freshwater prawns, with extremely long and fragile-looking forelimbs. They occur in streams from sea level to middle altitudes and are collected as food; several species probably occur here. Freshwater streams also support small, clear, freshwater shrimps *Caridinia* spp., which are active at night.

Myriapods – Millipedes and Centipedes

Tropical millipedes and centipedes can be very large and Seychelles contains a giant species of each, as well as many smaller species. Millipedes have two pairs of legs on each body segment and move forwards relatively slowly. Centipedes have only one pair of legs per segment and are much faster-moving predators.

Seychelles Giant Millipede *Seychelleptus seychellarum*

Milpat | Length to 30cm | Endemic
Found: granitics

Adults of this species are glossy dark brown-black while juveniles are bright red-brown. The giant millipede is a harmless vegetarian that relies on its tough cuticle and irritating chemical defence to protect it from predators. It feeds on leaf litter and other plant material and is mainly nocturnal. Once found on all islands of the granitic group, it is now most abundant on seabird islands free of introduced predators.

Giant Centipede *Scolopendra subspinipes*

Sanpye or Sanpye Ble | Length to 25cm | ?Native
Found: granitics | corallines | Aldabra

A very large centipede found throughout the tropics. Juveniles are blue-grey in colour while adults are orange-brown. It is mainly a nocturnal predator, hiding by day under leaf litter or bark. It overcomes its prey using poison injected by the powerful fangs; it can take lizards as well as invertebrates and can inflict a very painful bite. It is abundant on the plateaux of granitic islands and throughout the corallines.

Arachnids – Spiders, Scorpions, Whip Spiders, etc.

Most arachnids have eight legs; most obvious are the spiders (order Araneae), with at least 228 species recorded. There are only three true 'tarantulas' (suborder Mygalomorpha, family Theraphosidae) in Seychelles, and these are rarely seen. The true spiders (suborder Araneomorpha) are much more diverse and include some large web-building species and the free-roaming, rather tarantula-like huntsman spiders (family Sparassidae). The scorpions (order Scorpiones) are active hunters with well-developed pincers (pedipalps) and a poison sting in the tail. Three species occur in Seychelles. The whip spiders (subclass Amblypygi) are rather spider-like creatures with long legs, the first pair developed into exceptionally long feelers. There are two species in Seychelles.

Palm Spider *Nephila inaurita*

Bib | Leg span 8cm (female) | ?Native
Found: granitics | corallines | Aldabra

This large spider is virtually ubiquitous in Seychelles. The female sits at the centre of a large web built from heavy strands of silk, some of them yellow. The males are smaller. Small spiders of other species may occasionally be found living around the periphery of the web.

Argiope spp.

Bib | Length 2cm, Leg span 6cm | Native
Found: granitics | Aldabra

An attractive web-building spider with yellow and white stripes across the abdomen. Two species of *Argiope* occur in the Seychelles, *A. anasuja* and *A. trifasciata*. They build their webs in low vegetation, for example on some of the granitic islands, and both are abundant on the small seabird island of Récif.

Huntsman or Giant Crab Spider *Damastes validus (Rhitymna valida)*

Bib | Leg span to 12cm | Endemic
Found: granitics | corallines

This endemic species is one of seven representatives of the family Sparassidae in Seychelles. The sparassids are generally large, hairy spiders and one introduced species *Heteropoda venatoria* is common in houses. *D. validus* is a very large species – it does not build a web but uses silk to make a cylindrical shelter of living leaves. The individual photographed was found in a retreat made of rolled Takamaka leaves. This is a relatively common endemic, distributed throughout the granitics and some of the low coralline islands.

Giant Black Scorpion   *Chiromachus ochropus*

Skorpion Nwanr | Length to 10cm | Native
Found: granitics; Frégate

A large brown-black terrestrial scorpion, generally nocturnal and sheltering under rocks by day. It is a near-endemic, with a restricted range outside Seychelles – it has been recorded on Round Island, Mauritius and Zanzibar, but the current status of these populations is unknown. In Seychelles, it has been recorded on Frégate, Praslin and Récif, but the latter two populations may be extinct. An impressive scorpion, but not harmful; it is less likely to sting than the other two species found in Seychelles, and the sting is apparently less painful. Males (*a*) have a thin abdomen; that of females (*b*) is broader.

Two other species of scorpion are found in Seychelles. The more common is *Isometrus maculatus*, the Lesser Brown, or Spotted House, Scorpion. This is a widespread introduced species, transported around the tropics by humans. It reaches 5cm in length and is yellow-brown in colour with darker brown markings on the dorsal surface. It is found on many islands in the granitics and some of the Amirantes, in natural or artificial habitats (even houses), and can give a very painful sting.

The endemic *Lychas braueri* is a rarely seen brown arboreal scorpion found on Mahé, Praslin and Silhouette.

Tailless Whipscorpion   *Phrynichus scaber*

Tarantin Arme | Body length 2.5cm, Legspan 24cm, Whips to 15cm | Native
Found: granitics; predator-free islands

This large whip spider species is apparently restricted to predator-free seabird islands of the granitic Seychelles including Aride, Cousin, Cousine and possibly Frégate, although it was formerly found throughout the granitic archipelago. It is nocturnal, spending the day in dark, humid retreats, for example, under rocks, in shearwater burrows, wells and abandoned buildings. The large spiny pedipalps are used for capturing prey, mainly invertebrates such as crickets. The 'whips' are sensory limbs used to locate the prey. Although fearsome-looking, it is harmless to humans; amblypygids do not produce poison. The animals have an elaborate courtship dance that may last 5–8 hours. Like scorpions, females carry the newly hatched young on their backs. They are long-lived animals – related species can reach about 10 years – but are slow to reach maturity. Another, smaller species, *Charinus seychellarum*, is found throughout the granitics.

Insects

ORDER ODONATA – DRAGONFLIES AND DAMSELFLIES   The Odonata have aquatic larvae and adults that are active, winged predators. Dragonflies have fast-flying adults that normally perch with their wings outstretched. Adult damselflies are smaller, thinner-bodied insects with a relatively weak, fluttery flight. At rest, they hold their wings folded behind the body.

Orange Damselfly   *Ceriagrion glabrum*

Sigal | Length 3.5cm | Native
Found: granitics | corallines

The males of this damselfly are orange, females more green-brown in colour; both sexes have green eyes. In Seychelles it is found throughout the granitic islands, particularly on marshy coastal plateaux and on at least one of the low coralline islands.

Blue-tailed Damselfly   *Ischnura senegalensis*

Sigal | Length 3.5cm | Native
Found: granitics | corallines | Aldabra

A common and widespread damselfly in the granitic islands, where it occurs in plateau marshes. Larvae can tolerate some salinity and this species also occurs on coralline islands where there is standing water, including Denis and Aldabra Atoll.

Chalky Percher   *Diplacodes trivialis*

Sigal | Length 4.5cm | Native
Found: granitics

Males of this species have a powder-blue thorax and abdomen, the abdomen with a black tip. Females and newly emerged males have a black abdomen with yellow-green spots.

Phantom Flutterer   *Rhyothemis semihyalina*

Sigal | Length 5cm | Native
Found: granitics | corallines; Coëtivy | Aldabra; Assumption

A medium-sized dragonfly with dark body and basal patches on its hind wings, which reflect pink and green light. A common species at low altitudes on the granitic islands, and also found on coralline islands.

ORDER DICTYOPTERA – COCKROACHES An ancient order of insects with flattened, leaflike bodies. Several native species in Seychelles in addition to a range of species distributed by humans.

American Cockroach *Periplaneta americana*
Kankrela Later | Length to 4cm | Introduced
Found: granitics | corallines | Aldabra

A large red-brown cockroach, often found around human settlements. Originating in Africa, this species now has near-worldwide distribution thanks to humans. Mainly active at night, when it will fly to lights. It is an opportunistic scavenger, feeding on all sorts of organic matter. The similar Australian Cockroach *P. australasiae* is slightly smaller, usually darker in colour with pale stripes on the outer edge of the wings.

ORDER ISOPTERA – TERMITES Termites are social insects and are the only insects able to digest cellulose, thanks to symbiotic protozoa or fungi in the gut.

Nasutitermes spp.
Karya | Length to 5mm | Native
Found: granitics | corallines | Aldabra

Termites of this genus build a large, dark brown clay nest on tree and palm trunks at low altitudes, with roofed 'corridors' coming off the main nest to protect foraging workers. Each colony has a single king and queen, and swarms of winged males and females are periodically produced. Termite colonies are important decomposers of vegetable matter.

ORDER MANTODEA – MANTIDS Mantids are 'sit-and-wait' predators; most are camouflaged among vegetation and rely on keen eyesight to detect the movements of insects, ambushed with a strike of the armoured raptorial forelimbs.

Polyspilota aeruginosa
Seval-d-bwa | Length to 10cm | Native
Found: granitics | corallines | Aldabra

Two species of praying mantis occur in the granitic islands; this is the more common one in mid-altitude forests. Winged adults often come to light, especially in August–October. They are usually predominantly brown or grey shades, with two pale brown eyespots on the forewings. This species is also widely distributed in Africa and may have been introduced. The closely related endemic mantis *P. seychelliana* is usually all green with grey-brown eyespots, with a broad abdomen and larger head than this species. It tends to occur at higher altitudes in endemic vegetation on Mahé and Silhouette.

ORDER PHASMATODEA – PHASMIDS (STICK AND LEAF INSECTS)

The stick insects are elongate, green or brown stick-like herbivores related to the Orthoptera. The leaf insects also find safety through camouflage, but in their case they are disguised as segments of plant leaves. There are five species of stick insect and one leaf insect in Seychelles, all restricted to the larger granitic islands and all but one endemic.

Carausius gardineri

Seval-d-bwa | Length (body) to 6cm | Endemic
Found: granitics

The smallest of the endemic *Carausius* species. It is predominantly mid-brown with reddish eyes and patches of pale buff-brown. Females have a relatively broad body while males are thinner. The species feeds on several native fern species on the largest of the granitic islands.

Carausius alluaudi

Seval-d-bwa | Length (body) to 10cm (female) | Endemic
Found: granitics

Feeds on a range of plant species, including the introduced tree *Tabebuia pallida*, and native *Canthium bibracteatum* and *Dracaena reflexa*. Females are brown in colour and relatively wide-bodied, but many males are bright orange-red. *C. alluaudi* is found on most of the large islands. The similar *C. sechellensis* feeds only on ferns, favouring the abundant Ladder or Boston Fern *Nephrolepis biserrata*. Females are slightly larger than those of *C. alluaudi* and males are usually brown. It is found on all four large islands in addition to Félicité and Conception.

Leaf Insect *Phyllium bioculatum*

Mous Fey | Length to 8cm | ?Native
Found: granitics

Unlike all other Seychelles' stick insects, this species is primarily found on introduced trees and shrubs including Jamblon *Syzygium cumini*, Guava *Psidium guajava* and related plants, in the coastal lowlands and at mid-altitudes. The Leaf Insect is heavily camouflaged to resemble a leaf, with the limbs flattened with scalloped edges. In the adult female, even the wings are leaflike, and cannot be used in flight; the smaller, thinner male has functional, transparent wings. *Phyllium bioculatum* is a widespread Asian species, although Seychelles' individuals appear to show consistent differences to Asian forms. Historical records of leaf insects in Seychelles are confusing; different scientists have identified four different species of *Phyllium* here, although it seems unlikely that there has ever been more than one or two.

ORDER ORTHOPTERA – GRASSHOPPERS AND CRICKETS Orthoptera is a large, diverse order of insects including grasshoppers, locusts, bush crickets, crickets and groundhoppers. Many use sound for communication, especially at night. In natural habitats of the Seychelles, this is among the most prominent of insect groups.

Mole Cricket *Gryllotalpa* sp.

Length 2.6cm | Native
Found: granitics

This species is superbly adapted for burrowing underground. Its front limbs are modified like shovels to dig through earth; it feeds on roots. At night, it may be seen above the surface and is sometimes attracted to lights in houses. It is commonest at low altitudes in cultivated areas.

Odontolakis sp.

Length (body) 5–6cm | Endemic
Found: granitics; Mahé, Silhouette

A giant bush cricket with antennae several times the body length. Nymphs (*left*) are bright green, adults (*right*) become brown with long wings. Insects are active at night, when males give a simple high-pitched call similar to that of a cicada. *Odontolakis* feeds on the tough leaves of endemic palms and can give a powerful bite if handled.

Enoplotettix gardineri

Length to 4cm | Endemic
Found: granitics; Mahé, Praslin, Silhouette, Curieuse

This grasshopper species is bright green, and adults have wings striped in yellow and dark purple. The long, slender tibia of each hind leg is either bright blue (in the male) or red (in the female). It feeds on endemic palms and occurs on the larger granitic islands.

Monkey Grasshopper *Euschmidtia cruciformis*

Length to 2.1cm (female), 1.5cm (male) | Endemic
Found: granitics; Mahé and Silhouette

A flightless endemic that feeds on a variety of native and introduced trees and shrubs in mid-altitude forest, scrub and glacis on the larger islands. It is easily identified by its cross-shaped body: when at rest, the legs are held at right angles to the abdomen. The female is larger than the male.

Pelerinus rostratus

Length to 4.6cm | Endemic
Found: granitics | corallines; Denis

This bush cricket feeds on a variety of native and introduced trees including *Terminalia catappa*. *Pelerinus* adults often fly to house lights at night. It is found on the larger granitic islands and also Denis, where it was probably introduced.

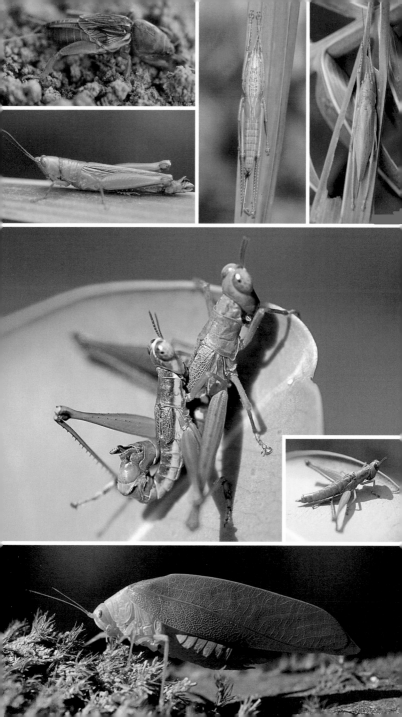

ORDER HEMIPTERA – BUGS The bugs are distinguished from other insect orders by their piercing mouthparts, which are generally used to feed on plant juices.

Pulvinaria urbicola
Lipou Blan | Length to 6mm | Introduced
Found: corallines; Bird

A small, sap-sucking scale insect, found on Bird island and probably other islands in the Seychelles, where it feeds on the sap of a range of plants including the tree *Pisonia grandis*. It is tended by ants that protect the bugs from predators and harvest sweet honeydew, produced by the bugs as a waste product. Many related species occur in Seychelles, including some important introduced pests.

Water Stick Insect *Ranatra grandocula*
Seval Dibwadelo | Length to 4cm | Native
Found: granitics

A distinctive elongate water bug, found in streams and pools from the coastal plateau to mid-altitudes. It lurks among cover, ambushing small aquatic creatures caught using its forelimbs. The animal lives underwater, breathing by means of a 'snorkel' from the rear of the body.

ORDER DIPTERA – FLIES The flies differ from most insects in that they have only one pair of wings (most insects have two pairs). Adults of some species are a nuisance; these pests include several mosquito species and the Sand Fly *Leptoconops spinosifrons*, a tiny biting midge less than 2mm long with brown-black head and thorax and white abdomen. Sand Flies are common on certain beaches and cause annoying bites on exposed skin, especially on the lower legs.

Drosophila sechellia
Mous Fri | Length 3mm | Endemic
Found: granitics | corallines; Denis (possibly others)

The family *Drosophilidae* (fruitflies) includes at least 37 species in Seychelles, about 40 per cent of them endemic. Some introduced species, such as the Mediterranean Fruit Fly *Ceratitis capitata*, are pests of cultivated fruit. *D. sechellia* is a tiny endemic fly, and feeds only on the fruit of the coastal shrub *Morinda citrifolia*. More than 150 different chemicals have been identified in ripe *Morinda* fruit, including acids highly toxic to most *Drosophila* species but tolerated by *D. sechellia*. It appears widespread on the granitic islands and Denis, and may also occur on other coralline islands.

ORDER COLEOPTERA – BEETLES Beetles are the most diverse group of animals on earth, with over 300,000 known species; about a third of all animal species are beetles. Beetles are characterised by their hardened forewings or elytra, which usually cover the abdomen and protect the second pair of transparent, flying wings beneath. In Seychelles, there at least 450 species, including many attractive diurnal species as well as the nocturnal firefly *Luciola laeta*.

Rhinoceros Beetle *Oryctes monoceros*
Bef Banan or Bef Koko | Length to 5cm | ?Native
Found: granitics | corallines | Aldabra

The largest beetle in Seychelles. The huge white larvae feed on Coconut Palms, mainly in dead stems and at the growing point of living (usually sick or weakened) plants. The adult beetles are huge and dark brown to black. Adults regularly fly to lights at night. The male (*a*) has a large projection on its head, like a rhino's horn, but this is absent in females (*b*). This was once an important pest species and although the area under coconut plantation has decreased, it is still abundant, feeding on the tissues of ageing or fallen palms.

Flower Scarab *Protaetia aurichalcea*
Makabe | Length to 1.5cm | Native
Found: granitics | corallines | Aldabra

A distinctive diurnal beetle found on the granitic and many coralline islands, as well as India and other Indian Ocean islands; it is especially abundant in coastal areas and gardens where adults frequent Papaya and other fruiting plants. They fly rather noisily between fruiting trees. The wing cases are a shiny metallic colour with white markings, while the thorax has large marginal white patches.

Olenecamptus bilobus
Makabe | Body length 1.5-2cm | Native
Found: granitics

The family Cerambycidae (longhorn beetles) includes species that live their larval stages in dead wood, twigs and reeds. The adult beetles have long antennae and extremely powerful jaws. One endemic species appeared to be closely associated with the endemic tree *Vateriopsis seychellarum*, which is now very rare, and may be extinct. *Olenecamptus bilobus* is a small but attractively marked species, found on the granitic islands in gardens and forests.

Green-lined Longhorn Beetle *Xystrocera globosa*

Makabe | Length (body) to 3cm | Introduced

Found: granitics

 A larger longhorn beetle species that often comes to lights in buildings at night. The female lays her eggs in crevices in the bark of Albizzia *Paraserianthes falcataria*, and the larvae feed by boring galleries beneath the bark.

Father Philibert's Beetle *Calirrhiphis philiberti*

Makabe Plim | Length (body) to 2cm | Endemic

Found: granitics | corallines

 An attractive endemic beetle that has survived on many of the granitic islands, in woodland, gardens and plantations from the coastal plain to high altitudes. The nocturnal adult has large much-divided antennae to 1.5cm long and is attracted to lights at night. The larva feeds on dead wood of various tree species.

Frégate Island Giant Tenebrionid Beetle *Polposipus herculeanus*

Bib Arme | Length 2.5–3cm | Endemic

Found: granitics; Frégate

 Although it was probably more widely distributed in the past, this species is now found only on Frégate – there is also a small population in captivity in the UK. The flightless, long-legged adult is a large grey-brown beetle, usually found in clusters on the bark of Sandragon and other rough-barked trees. It can be recognised by its round abdomen and the raised tubercles on the wing cases. Larvae feed on the wood of Sandragon and various other trees.

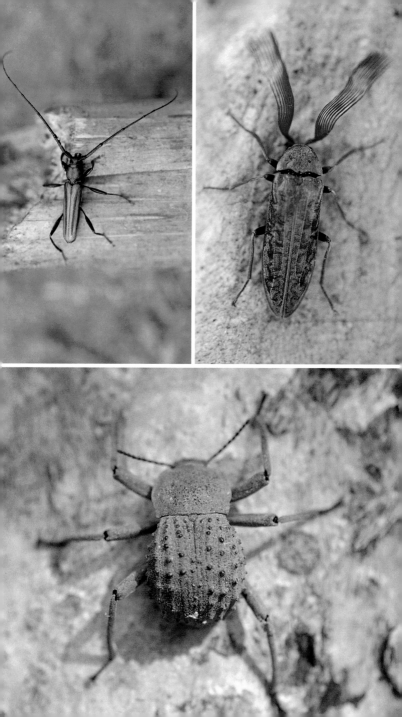

ORDER LEPIDOPTERA – BUTTERFLIES AND MOTHS In the granitic and low coralline islands, there are few butterfly species, but there is a greater diversity on the raised atolls of the Aldabra group.

BUTTERFLIES

Eggfly *Hypolimnas misippus*
Papiyon | Wingspan 6cm | Native
Found: granitics | corallines | Aldabra

The Eggfly shows sexual dimorphism; the female (*a*) mimics the poisonous African Monarch Butterfly (*Danaus chrysippus*), deriving protection from predators through its similarity to the toxic species. Males (*b*) are glossy blue-black with prominent blue-edged white spots on each wing. The Eggfly adult is most common in the wet season from December–March. The larger species *H. bolina* also occurs in Seychelles.

African Grass Blue *Zizeeria knysna*
Papiyon Ble | Wingspan 2cm | ?Introduced
Found: granitics | corallines | Aldabra

The wings of this tiny butterfly are purplish-blue in males, brown in females. The underside is silver-grey with small black spots. The similar *Zizula hylax* is slightly smaller (1.8cm) with an additional dark spot on the underside of the forewing. Both species fly very close to the ground. Larvae feed on a range of small herbs, including *Desmodium* and *Amaranthus*.

Seychelles Milkweed Butterfly *Euploea mitra*
Papiyon | Wingspan 6.5cm | Endemic
Found: granitics; Mahé, Silhouette

An endemic butterfly species that belongs to a genus (*Euploea*) almost entirely restricted to Asia. Adults of this species are occasionally seen, usually as solitary individuals, in hill woodland on Mahé and Silhouette. The larval food-plant is not known, but is probably a member of the plant family Asclepiadaceae or Apocynaceae.

Evening Brown *Melanitis leda*
Papiyon Gri or Papiyon Tourtel | Wingspan 6cm | Native
Found: granitics

This large, brown butterfly is active in the late afternoon, evening, and early morning. It occurs throughout the granitic islands in woodland, scrub and waste places. The upperside is a dark chestnut brown with red-brown on the forewing. The underside has stippled brown markings, with small eyespots. The caterpillar feeds on grasses. It is green with two prominent horns near the head.

Aldabra White Butterfly *Belenois aldabrensis* (*Teracolus aldabrensis*)

Papiyon | Wingspan 3.5cm | Endemic
Found: Aldabra; Aldabra, Assumption, Astove
An endemic white butterfly. The larval host plant is believed to be *Morinda citrifolia*.

Blue Pansy *Junonia orithya madagascariensis* (*Precis o. m.*)

Papiyon Ble | Wingspan 4cm | Native
Found: Aldabra; Aldabra, Assumption, Cosmoledo
A beautiful butterfly restricted in Seychelles to the Aldabra group. The larvae feed on plants in the family Acanthaceae.

Moths

Cordia Moth *Ethmia nigroapicella*

Lay | Wingspan 1.5cm | Native
Found: granitics | corallines | Aldabra
A tiny moth, with brown forewings; the hind wings (normally hidden) are orange with black tips. The caterpillars feed on *Cordia subcordata*.

Crimson Speckled Footman or Heliotrope Moth
Utetheisa pulchelloides

Lay | Wingspan 3cm | Native

Found: granitics | corallines | Aldabra
A white day-flying moth with red and black speckles on the wings. The small orange-brown caterpillars feed on the leaves of *Tournefourtia*, a plant of the beach crest.

Death's Head Hawkmoth *Acherontia atropos*

Lay Tetdemor | Wingspan 10–13cm | Native
Found: granitics

Adult Death's Head Hawkmoths have a skull-like pale marking on the black thorax. The larvae (*inset*) of this species are equally distinctive; extremely large (up to 13cm long) and yellow with pale blue diagonal markings on the sides and a short blunt tail. The caterpillar feeds on a variety of plant species including *Stachytarpheta* spp. and *Tabebuia pallida*.

Oleander Hawkmoth *Daphnis nerii*

Lay | Wingspan to 11cm | Native
Found: granitics

A rarely seen native hawkmoth. The adult is attractively marked in green and pink. The larva, which is predominantly yellow or green, feeds on Oleander (*Nerium oleander*) and related plants, and are often abundant, completely defoliating groups of trees, or all the trees on an island.

Order Hymenoptera – Wasps, Bees and Ants

Carpenter Bee *Xylocopa caffra*
Mous Brinzil | Length 1.8-2.0cm | Native
Found: granitics | corallines | Aldabra

Female Carpenter Bees are predominantly black with distinct bands of bright yellow hairs. In males, the upperside of the body is covered with yellow hairs. Both sexes have dark brown wings that reflect metallic hues. Carpenter Bees nest in burrows in dry wood where they lay eggs on stores of pollen. The species is widespread in Africa.

African Honey Bee *Apis mellifera*
Mous d Myel | Length 1.2-1.5cm | Introduced
Found: granitics | corallines

The honeybee was probably introduced to Seychelles by early settlers. Now, it occurs throughout the granitic islands and on some of the coralline islands. This species is widespread in Africa.

Yellow, or Paper, Wasp *Polistes olivaceus*
Mous Zonn | Length 1-2cm | ?Native
Found: granitics | corallines

This yellow and black social wasp builds a paper nest under sheltering foliage. Nests start small with a few cells, but can grow to 30cm across, with a single layer of brood cells on the flat underside. Wasps defend the nest aggressively and have a painful sting.

Seychelles Potter Wasp *Delta alluaudi*
Mous Mason | Length 2-2.5cm | Endemic
Found: granitics | corallines; Denis (perhaps others)

A large black and orange solitary wasp. The brood chambers (picture), built from mud on rocks and buildings, resemble neatly turned pots around 2cm across. Each chamber is provisioned with paralysed caterpillars before a single egg is laid, after which the chamber is sealed with mud. An endemic species of the granitic islands, introduced to Denis and perhaps other coralline islands.

Mud Dauber Wasp *Sceliphron fuscum*
Mous Mason | Length 2-2.5cm | Native
Found: granitics | corallines

A large, solitary black wasp. The brood chambers are usually constructed in a connected line, often on the underside of young palm leaves. The adult collects spiders to provision the brood chamber.

Vegetation

The vegetation of Seychelles has changed greatly since the islands were first colonized. Originally, the granitic islands were clothed in forest or scrub, with moist mossy forests at higher altitudes on the largest islands, mid-altitude forests dominated by endemic tree species such as the dipterocarp *Vateriopsis seychellarum* (now extremely rare), and marshy coastal 'plateaux' fringed by salt-tolerant shrubs and trees including mangrove and beach-crest vegetation. The flora of low-lying coralline islands would have been much more species-poor, dominated by widespread plants dispersed by ocean currents and tolerant of salt spray and drought. The raised coral atolls, of greater antiquity, would have supported many endemic species as they do today, with dense scrub and some unique habitats including grasslands maintained by tortoise grazing.

Habitats Today – Granitic Islands

Habitats on the larger granitic islands can best be divided by altitude. Altitude has an important effect on seasonal availability of water, humidity, temperature, and other factors which influence plants. There are no absolute 'cut-off' points; there is usually a transition from one vegetation zone to another, and the altitude of the zone boundaries will depend on the location of a site; places exposed to incoming cloud (i.e. north-west facing slopes) may support moist forest vegetation at lower altitudes.

MOIST FOREST ZONE 500-900M The highest altitudes on the islands of Mahé and Silhouette are often wreathed in cloud while lower altitudes are clear. The annual rainfall is much higher than at sea level, and precipitation more evenly distributed through the year. Temperatures are also lower, causing slower loss of water. These high altitudes have also been least exploited by humans, allowing some rare endemics to survive. Mist forests (*a*) are often dominated by the endemic tree *Northea* (Kapisen) with a range of other endemics and introduced species. On cliffs and hilltops, *Northea* can be very stunted, only a few metres tall. The branches are festooned with deep growth of moss and other epiphytic plants.

Open, rocky cliffs known as glacis (*b*) support many endemic species at high altitudes.

MID-ALTITUDES 100–500M Mid-altitude forests are less constantly humid than the highest forests, but have many small streams, with their own characteristic marginal vegetation of palms and *Pandanus*. On Praslin, Curieuse and part of Mahé, mid-altitudes are dominated by endemic palm forests (*c*) – Coco de Mer on Praslin, other endemic species on Mahé. Elsewhere on Praslin, Mahé and Silhouette, these forests are dominated by introduced tree species, particularly Cinnamon.

At mid-altitudes, humans have replaced forests with plantations of Santol, Mahogany and Tea. In drier locations (parts of Praslin, Curieuse and south Mahé), eroded red-earth soils at mid-altitudes support scrub that often contains endemic shrubs and palms as well as introduced shrubs. Glacis also occurs – sometimes invaded by introduced species including the Cocoplum, in other places supporting endemics like the Jellyfish Tree.

COASTAL LOWLANDS 0–10M The flat coastal lowlands (plateaux) differ geologically from the granite hills, being relatively recent (less than 10,000 years old) and made up largely of reef-derived sediments. Plateau forest made up of native trees, once probably dominant here, is now very rare on the larger islands; some good examples survive on La Digue (dominated by *Calophyllum* and *Terminalia* (*d*)), with fragments on Mahé and Praslin. Freshwater marshes (*e*) have also mostly been lost, although most of the larger granite islands still have some marshland. Through most of the 20th century, coconut plantations (*f*) covered most of the plateau areas and all of some small islands. Now, these are uneconomic and have been turned to other uses (particularly urban development) or allowed to become overgrown scrub. Urban areas, gardens, grasslands and waste ground make up a significant part of the land use of these coastal areas. Some of these vegetation types extend onto the low granite hills, although where undisturbed the 'mid-altitude forest' type vegetation may cover granitic slopes to 10m above sea level.

LITTORAL ZONE The narrow coastal zone supports several distinctive vegetation types, most of which are composed of species capable of marine dispersal and with a wide distribution outside Seychelles. In silty areas flooded by the high tide, mangroves (*g*) occur. On the beach crest above sandy beaches and (sometimes) rocky shores, beach-crest vegetation (*h*) is found. In the sea itself, seagrass beds are made up of flowering plants that have returned to a fully marine existence.

SMALLER ISLANDS The smaller granitic islands (*i*) are generally fairly low, and are drier than the larger high islands. In their vegetation, they have much in common with the coralline outer islands. Many were formerly completely covered with coconut plantations, with the exception of glacis on dry, open hilltops. Today, these plantations are overgrown with mainly

introduced vegetation on many islands (e.g. Marianne and Grande Soeur). A few islands (notably Aride, Cousin) have been restored to native-dominated woodland and scrub. The very smallest islands tend to support only tough, salt-tolerant herbs, with a few windswept shrubs and trees.

Coralline Islands

LOW CORALLINE ISLANDS Most of the
coralline islands (*j*) suffered a similar fate to
the smaller granitic islands, with much of
the original vegetation being lost, first for
the mining of guano (seabird droppings,
used as fertilizer) and then for coconut
plantations. Most are still dominated by
coconut plantations with thick re-growth of
palms and some native trees like *Pisonia* and
Morinda. On many islands, Coconuts were
interplanted with casuarinas and in places
casuarina woodlands have formed. Around
the coasts, a band of beach-crest vegetation
usually survives, with shrubs and trees
including *Scaevola*, *Tournefourtia*, *Cordia* and
Guettarda. Freshwater wetlands are rare on
coral islands, although Denis has marshes
with *Typha* and *Acrostichum*. Mangrove
habitat occurs in the sheltered lagoons of

atolls. The large shrub *Pemphis* (absent from the granitic islands) may
grow on the beach crest or in the edge of lagoons. Where ground-nesting
seabirds are prominent, as on Bird Island and Desnoeufs, breeding
grounds are dominated by a low herb mat made up of a small number of
grass, herb and sedge species. Many coralline islands today have hotels
and airstrips, with large parts of the islands given over to grassy open
habitats and gardens, mainly of exotic ornamental plants.

RAISED CORALLINE ISLANDS Aldabra and nearby atolls and islands are
older than the low coral islands and support a wider range of habitats and
some endemic species. However, on all raised coralline islands with the
exception of Aldabra itself, natural terrestrial habitats were destroyed by
the mining of guano deposits in the 19th and 20th centuries. Mangrove is
extensive within the lagoons of Aldabra (800ha), Cosmoledo and Astove,
while freshwater bodies only occur on Aldabra. Beach-crest scrub (mainly
Scaevola) also occurs. On Aldabra in particular, extensive stands of
Pemphis scrub occur, with more species-rich mixed scrub in places,
including species like *Sideroxylon*, *Euphorbia*, *Ficus* and *Canthium*. There
are even small areas of broadleaf woodland like the Takamaka grove
(*Calophyllum*). Aldabra also has grassland including single-species coastal
Sporobolus virginicus grassland and tortoise turf, a low natural lawn
maintained by grazing and made up of 22 herb and grass species, some
endemic, many of which are genetically dwarfed.

Mangrove Habitats

Mangrove habitats are dominated by a small number of trees and shrubs adapted to survive the extreme conditions at the edge of the sea. Most have 'breathing roots' called pneumatophores, which are aerial portions of roots used to aerate the remainder of the root system, buried in anoxic sediments. The granitic islands and Aldabra have extensive areas of mangrove.

White Mangrove *Avicennia marina*
Mangliye Blan | Height 6m | Native

Found: granitics; Mahé, Praslin, Silhouette, La Digue, Curieuse, Marianne, Thérèse, Cousin | corallines; Farquhar | Aldabra; Aldabra, Cosmoledo, Astove

The most widespread and common mangrove of the granitic islands. A relatively small species, growing to 6m in height and spread. The pencil-like breathing roots rise vertically to a height of around 20cm from the mud beneath the tree. The small flowers develop into flattened fruit about 3cm across, covered with a grey-green felt-like outer skin (pericarp).

Bruguiera gymnorrhiza
Mangliye Lat | Height to 10m | Native

Found: granitics; Mahé, Praslin, Silhouette, Curieuse | Aldabra; Aldabra, Cosmoledo, Astove

A tree with ovate, glossy leaves up to 15cm long, and 'knee roots', short inverted 'V's of root emerging from the substrate some distance from the trunk. The propagules are elongate, up to 15cm long, with a persistent, much-divided spiky calyx at the top.

Red Mangrove *Rhizophora mucronata*
Mangliye Rouz, Mangliye Oban | Height to 15m | Native

Found: granitics; Mahé, Praslin, Silhouette, La Digue, Curieuse, Cousin, Récif | corallines; Amirantes (Poivre, St Joseph), Farquhar | Aldabra; Aldabra, Cosmoledo, Astove

This widespread species has large glossy leaves and arching stilt roots descending from the central stem. The fruits germinate on the tree, forming spear-shaped green propagules up to 50cm long. When ripe, they fall to earth. Those that fall at low water may lodge securely in an upright position in the mud, where they can grow. Of those that fall at high tide most probably die after being cast up on the beach.

Sonneratia alba
Mangliye Fler | Height to 15m | Native

Found: granitics; Mahé, Praslin, Silhouette | Aldabra; Aldabra, Cosmoledo (very rare)

This tall mangrove has stiff, rounded leaves. The beautiful, ephemeral flowers are a mass of white stamens, and open at night. The fruits (*see* photo) are green and rounded, about 3cm across, with persistent calyx segments. The pneumatophores are upright conical structures.

Beach Crest

At the top of sandy beaches, and sometimes also rocky shores, a distinctive assemblage of shrubs and trees occurs. Most are native, although widely distributed outside Seychelles as their fruits and seeds are adapted for marine dispersal.

👑 *Boerhavia repens*

Patat Oven | Spreading stems to 70cm; height 30cm | Native
Found: granitics; Aride, Cousin, other small islands | corallines; Bird, Denis, Amirantes (Desnoeufs, D'Arros, St Joseph), Farquhar | Aldabra

A short, spreading herb found on the coral islands and coastal plateaux of some granitic islands. It has small rounded leaves and heads of tiny white or pinkish flowers. Several similar, related species occur.

👑 Spider Lily *Hymenocallis littoralis*

Lis Bord-d-mer | Leaves 50–70cm | Introduced
Found: granitics; most medium-large islands | corallines; many islands

This introduced bulbous plant is widely naturalized in coastal places. It grows in dense clumps, with long, strap-like leaves, which wither in very dry spells. In the wet season, the white flowers are produced, in a cluster borne on an upright stem. Each flower has a central flared daffodil-like trumpet, from which six long stamens radiate, the anthers bearing yellow pollen. Behind the funnel, there are six narrow drooping perianth segments.

🌿 Dodder or Love Vine *Cassytha filiformis*

Lalyann San Fen | Stems to 3m | Native
Found: granitics | corallines | Aldabra

A leafless, rootless, parasitic liana. It consists of a spaghetti-like tangle of yellow or reddish stems climbing through grasses, herbs or shrubs, usually in coastal areas. The twining stems connect to the host plant at points where they touch, obtaining food and water from the host. The tiny flowers are followed by whitish globular berries.

🌿 Beach Morning Glory *Ipomoea pes-caprae*

Patatran | Stems to 5m | Native
Found: granitics | corallines | Aldabra

A widespread liana of coastal areas, usually forming a mat of creeping stems at the beach crest, often colonising bare sand. It also occasionally occurs inland. The leaves are notched at the tip, and the flared, trumpet-like flowers are pink. This species occurs in coastal areas throughout the tropics.

Casuarina or Beefwood *Casuarina equisetifolia*
Sed | Height to 30m | ?Introduced
Found: granitics | corallines | Aldabra

Casuarina can rapidly grow into a very large tree. It is widely planted throughout the tropics to control coastal erosion. Its foliage is light and feathery, made up of many jointed stems giving it the overall appearance of a conifer. The fruiting structures are dry, woody cone-like brown spheres around 1.5cm across. They litter the ground beneath Casuarinas and are painful if stepped on.

Alexandrian Laurel *Calophyllum inophyllum*
Takamaka | Height to 20m | Native
Found: granitics | corallines | Aldabra

Takamaka is a large tree with thick, fissured bark, dark green, glossy leaves, white flowers with a boss of yellow stamens, and hard, round, green fruit. It is valued for its dark reddish wood, which is used for furniture and boats. Although native to Seychelles, it has been much planted in the past for timber, as a shade tree and to control coastal erosion. Now, most beaches on the granitic islands have some large trees. The species also occurs away from beaches, reaching the summit of small islands, and has been planted at altitudes of 300m or more on Mahé. It also occurs on the coralline islands including Aldabra. A fungal disease of Takamaka has caused dieback or complete death of many trees in recent years.

Cordia *Cordia subcordata*
Porse | Height to 10m | Native
Found: granitics | corallines | Aldabra

An untidy small tree of the beach crest, with broad ovate leaves and bright orange flowers. The fruit are green, ripening to brown, ovoid or spherical hanging structures. The tree is often completely defoliated by attacks of the caterpillar of the moth *Ethmia nigroapicella* (*see* p.166).

Guettarda *Guettarda speciosa*
Bwa Kasan (Bor-d-mer) | Height to 8m | Native
Found: granitics | corallines | Aldabra

A small tree of the beach vegetation, with large, ovoid glossy leaves. The flowers are tubular, white and highly scented; they open at night and drop in the heat of the day. The fruit are white when ripe, and float; they are dispersed by the sea and the plant has a wide distribution including almost all islands of Seychelles.

Scaevola *Scaevola sericea*

Vouloutye | Height to 4m | Native

Found: granitics | corallines | Aldabra

The ubiquitous shrub of beach-crest vegetation, also occasionally found in other areas exposed to salt spray, such as low hillsides close to the sea. Scaevola is a spreading shrub with long, glossy, bright green leaves, white flowers with fanlike lower petals, and white berry-like fruit. In many places, it forms a hedge of stems at the beach crest.

Barringtonia or Fish Poison Tree *Barringtonia asiatica*

Bonnen Kare | Height to 15m | Native

Found: granitics; Mahé, Praslin, Silhouette, La Digue, Curieuse, Félicité, Frégate, North | corallines; Denis, Amirantes (where introduced)

An attractive coastal tree with very large, glossy leaves with short leaf stems. Young leaves often emerge reddish purple in colour, becoming deep glossy green later. The large white flowers usually open at night and have clusters of many long white stamens which drop to the ground beneath the tree in the day. The fruits are large and distinctive angular structures – square in cross-section – which can float and are dispersed by the sea. As a result *Barringtonia* is widely distributed throughout the Indopacific region, although in Seychelles it appears only native to the northern islands. It has been introduced to some of the Amirantes. The leaves produce a poison when crushed, and have been used by some Pacific islanders to kill fish, giving rise to one of the English names of this tree.

Tournefourtia argentea

Bwa Taba | Height to 5m | Native

Found: granitics; very rare, on exposed beaches | corallines | Aldabra

A widespread shrub of the beach crest, with velvety silver-haired leaves. It favours exposed sandy beaches growing on the seaward side of other shrubs such as Scaevola. A common plant on coralline islands but rare on the granitics – on Mahé, only present on one or two exposed beaches at the south of the island. On Bird island, some large old tree-like specimens (to 5m) occur in the midst of the Sooty Tern colony. This is the larval foodplant of the small day-flying moth *Utetheisa pulchelloides* (*see* p.166)

Hernandia *Hernandia nymphaeifolia*

Bwa Blan | Height to 20m | Native

Found: granitics; Mahé, Praslin, Silhouette, La Digue, Curieuse, Félicité, Frégate, North, Cousine | Aldabra; Astove (where introduced?)

A large tree that can be recognized by its large peltate ('lily-pad') leaves; the leaf stems join the leaf blade centrally, not at the margin. The scented flowers are followed by hanging fruit (inset) that look like Chinese lanterns, each consisting of a black ridged fruit surrounded by an inflated green-white cupule, for sea dispersal.

Hibiscus *Hibiscus tiliaceus*

Var | Height to 12m | Native

Found: granitics; Mahé, Praslin, Silhouette, La Digue, Curieuse, Félicité, Frégate, North | corallines; Denis, Amirantes (D'Arros, St Joseph) | Aldabra; Aldabra (where rare), Astove

An untidy, spreading small tree, with many near-horizontal branches and leaning trunks. Large, roughly hairy heart-shaped leaves. Flowers pale yellow with a dark maroon eye. Occurs at the top of beaches and in woodland and scrub on the coastal plateau or low hills.

Mahoe or Portia Oil Nut *Thespesia populnea*

Bwa-d-roz | Height to 8m | Native

Found: granitics; Mahé, Praslin, Silhouette, La Digue, Curieuse, Félicité, Frégate | corallines; Bird, Denis, Amirantes (D'Arros) | Aldabra; Aldabra

A small tree resembling *Hibiscus tiliaceus*, but with narrower, heart-shaped, hairless leaves. The new flowers are pale yellow, with red or maroon patches at the base of each petal; the whole flower becomes reddish purple with age. The similar species *T. populneoides* occurs on Aldabra.

Puzzle Nut *Xylocarpus moluccensis*

Mangliye Pasyans | Height to 8m | Native

Found: granitics; most islands | Aldabra; Aldabra, Cosmoledo

A small tree with pinnate leaves, consisting of 4–8 small, pointed, dark green leaflets, arranged in pairs. The fruit is an orange-sized sphere surrounded by green or brown pericarp, containing 6–12 large, irregularly shaped brown seeds. The seeds fit together like pieces of a three-dimensional jigsaw puzzle, giving the tree its English name. A second species, *X. granatum* (Mangliye Ponm), is found in mangrove areas; its fruit reach 25cm in diameter.

Freshwater Marsh

Freshwater marsh habitat is most extensive on coastal plateaux, for example on La Digue, where it grades into woodland. Even fairly small granitic islands may have a wetland area. On the coralline islands, freshwater habitats are rare.

♛ Water Hyacinth *Eichornia crassipes*

Height to 45cm | Introduced
Found: granitics; Mahé, La Digue

An attractive but ecologically damaging aquatic weed; floating plants are supported on the water surface by the swollen air-filled leaf bases. The flowers are large and mauve-blue. The plant can reproduce rapidly and has become a problem weed in the waterways of La Digue.

♛ Ludwigia *Ludwigia octovalvis*

Herb Lanmar | Height to 1.5m | Introduced
Found: granitics; almost all islands

A common herb of damp places and marshland, with upright stems bearing long, elliptical hairy leaves, each a few centimetres long, and yellow four-petalled flowers in the leaf axils.

♛ White Waterlily *Nymphaea lotus*

Lisdo | Flowers 15cm across; leaves 30cm | Introduced
Found: granitics; Mahé, Praslin, La Digue

The White Waterlily is common in lowland ponds on La Digue and parts of Mahé. This is a robust plant; its large floating leaves can cover sizeable stretches of open water. The more delicate blue-purple water lily *Nymphaea caerulea* (inset) is only found in cultivation.

♛ Water Lettuce *Pistia stratiotes*

Letilanmar | Rosettes to 30cm across; usually much less | Introduced
Found: granitics; Mahé, La Digue

A small, floating plant with a dense rosette of velvety leaves. Flowers are small and rarely seen but the species spreads rapidly through vegetative reproduction, and can quickly cover bodies of standing water, for example on La Digue plateau. Like the Water Hyacinth, it is an invasive weed.

♛ Bulrush *Typha javanica*

Zonk | Height to 2m | Native
Found: granitics; Mahé, Praslin, Silhouette, La Digue, Curieuse, North | corallines; Denis

A tall aquatic plant, with long, flattened blue-green leaves and cylindrical brown seed heads. Although primarily a freshwater species, it can tolerate some salinity in the water, and may be found in coastal marshes and mangrove on the granitic islands and Denis.

🌸 Pigyam *Alocasia macrorrhiza*
Vya | Height to 3m | Introduced
Found: granitics; Mahé, Praslin, Silhouette, La Digue, Curieuse, North, Aride, Cousin |
corallines; Denis, Amirantes (D'Arros)

A giant terrestrial herb, with huge glossy leaves held on stout leaf stems arising from a swollen rhizome. The corm and shredded leaf stems can be used to feed pigs, giving this plant its English name. In Seychelles, this species is found in wet woodland on the coastal plateau of most granitic islands, and on many of the coralline islands. It occasionally produces a cream-green, *Arum*-like inflorescence on a stem from the rhizome, but mainly appears to spread by vegetative means. The related Cocoyam *Colocasia esculenta* is a smaller marsh plant, with heart-shaped leaves on leaf stems to 1m. The leaf stems are sometimes deep purple in colour. Cocoyam produces an edible tuber and was once widely cultivated.

🌳 Badamier or Indian Almond *Terminalia catappa*
Bodanmyen | Height to 20m | Native
Found: granitics | corallines; almost all islands | Aldabra

A tall tree with a distinctive layered shape, especially obvious in young trees where the branches emerge horizontally from the straight central trunk in regular, well-spaced whorls like umbrella spokes. This is a widespread species, found in a variety of habitats from the coastal plateau to mid-altitudes, but especially abundant in marshy forest about sea level, e.g. on the plateau of La Digue. It also occurs on many coralline islands, including Denis, and on the Amirantes and Aldabra (where it has been planted). Badamier has large, simple leaves and is partially deciduous, the old leaves turning reddish-orange before they fall (main picture). Spikes of tiny greenish-yellow flowers are followed by large fleshy fruit, purple-red when ripe (inset). In Seychelles, the kernel of the central almond-like nut is eaten in sugary nougat. The 'nut' floats and the seed can germinate after immersion in the sea.

Low-altitude Forests

Woodland habitats were once extensive on the plateaux of granitic islands, and on some coralline islands; now they are much restricted in extent. On large islands, native low-altitude woodland is often dominated by *Calophyllum* and *Terminalia*; on small islands like Cousin and Aride, a range of native species occurs, particularly *Pisonia*.

Canavalia cathartica

Gro Pwa | Climbing stems to 10m | Native

Found: granitics | corallines; rare, e.g. Amirantes (D'Arros)

A widespread, rampant, climbing plant of the beach crest or coastal plateau woodland. Leaves with three rounded leaflets, flowers bright pink, pods broad and flattened, ripening to dark brown. The Shore Bean *Vigna marina* has *Canavalia*-like foliage and grows in similar coastal situations but has yellow flowers.

Ficus lutea

Lafous Gran Fey | Height to 15m | Native

Found: granitics | corallines; almost all islands | Aldabra

A potentially large fig tree found on granitic and coralline islands, with large, broad leaves up to 17cm long and 11cm wide, and yellowish fruit 2cm across. Several other native figs occur in Seychelles; all bear fig fruits directly from the stems, have white milky sap, and sometimes aerial roots. *Ficus reflexa* and *F. rubra* are found in lowland forests.

Looking-glass Tree *Heritiera littoralis*

Bwa-d-tab | Height to 20m | Native

Found: granitics; Mahé, Praslin, Silhouette, La Digue, Curieuse, North

Old specimens develop a thick trunk with flared buttresses. The upperside of the leaves is dark green; the underside has a shiny surface caused by its dense coat of silvery hairs, although the English name is hopelessly optimistic. The fruits are large, brown and woody, with a pronounced keel. The tree occurs in lowland and mid-altitude forests.

Morinda or Indian Mulberry *Morinda citrifolia*

Bwa Torti | Height to 5m | Native

Found: granitics | corallines; Denis

A small tree or shrub found in a wide range of habitats from glacis to beach crest. Cream-white tubular flowers emerge from a small green receptacle, which later develops into the distinctive fruit. The fruit is knobbed, becoming white or pale brown with a nauseating aroma when ripe. The soft flesh contains many black seeds and is eaten by tortoises. Cut leafy stems are used as browse for cattle and the oily, smelly fruit used as bait in fish traps.

Ochrosia *Ochrosia oppositifolia*
Bwa Sousouri | Height 10–15m | Native
Found: granitics; most islands | corallines; Denis, Amirantes

A tree with long, glossy leaves held in bunches at the tips of tiered branches arranged round the central trunk like umbrella spokes. The large ovoid fruits, yellow when ripe, are usually held in pairs and are eaten by bats and, after falling to the ground, by tortoises. The bark of this tree is used medicinally and it is highly valued; on populated islands trees often show signs of bark removal.

Pisonia or Cabbage Tree *Pisonia grandis*
Mapou | Height to 15m | Native
Found: granitics; seabird islands, Frégate, Aride, Cousin, Cousine, Récif, Mamelles | corallines; most islands | Aldabra

A native tree found on islands throughout the Indian Ocean and Pacific. It is dispersed by birds; the fruits, each a centimetre or so long, are coated with a natural glue. They adhere to the plumage of seabirds, which spread the seeds between islands. The sticky fruits are difficult to preen out of feathers, and unlucky birds with a heavy load of the fruits become clumsy and more likely to collect even more. Badly affected birds fall to the forest floor and die (inset). However, populations of seabirds on the predator-free islands where Pisonia occurs are large enough to sustain such losses. Pisonia has very poor, spongy timber. As the tree ages, it becomes increasingly unstable and rotten, and eventually falls. However, fallen trees often survive and send many new stems up to join the canopy. This strategy may help this fast-growing but short-lived tree to dominate plateau woodland on seabird islands. Pisonia is absent from the largest granitic islands. On Silhouette, the related endemic tree *P. sechellarum* occurs in a unique high-altitude forest formation. This species, with longer, more lanceolate leaves than *P. grandis*, was first described in 1986. There is also another indigenous *Pisonia* species on Aldabra: *P. aculeata*, a scrambling shrub.

Wright's Gardenia *Rothmannia annae*
Bwa Sitronn | Height to 7m | Endemic
Found: granitics; Aride

A small evergreen tree, with neat, glossy dark green foliage resembling citrus leaves, hence the Creole name. The beautiful flowers are highly scented. The fruit are large, ovoid or spherical, green and hard. In the wild, this species is restricted to the island of Aride, although it once occurred more widely in the granitic Seychelles group. It is cultivated in gardens on Mahé and some other islands.

Coconut Plantations, Gardens and Waste Ground

Coconut plantations once dominated the lowlands of most islands, but are now generally abandoned and overgrown. Gardens have a range of largely ornamental species, while waste ground supports more aggressive ornamentals, especially lianas, and former crop plants.

👑 *Asystasia* sp.

Manztou | Stem length to 1m | Introduced
Found: granitics | corallines | most islands

A widespread introduced species, originally used as a fodder for livestock, and now found in grassy areas, gardens and roadsides. Its long, sprawling stems terminate in spikes of small trumpet-shaped cream flowers. A second species of *Asystasia* occurs on the Aldabra group.

👑 Madagascar Periwinkle *Catharanthus roseus*

Roz Anmer | Height 50cm | Introduced
Found: granitics; most islands | corallines; most islands | Aldabra

A widespread medicinal plant, with bushy stems terminating in attractive pink or white flowers. Probably an early introduction to Seychelles and now found in gardens and on open glacis at low-mid altitudes throughout the archipelago.

👑 Sensitive Plant *Mimosa pudica*

Sansib | Stem length to 1m | Introduced
Found: granitics; most islands

A short, woody herb with spreading, spiny stems carrying groups of pinnate leaves, each with many narrow opposite leaflets. When touched, the leaflets rapidly collapse together and leaves fold down into their night-time position to protect them from herbivores. The flowers are small pink pompoms, followed by groups of spiny pods.

👑 *Senna occidentalis*

Kaspyant | Height to 1.5m | Introduced
Found: granitics; Praslin, North | corallines; Denis, Amirantes (D'Arros)

A tall herb, sometimes rather woody at the base. The five-petalled yellow flowers are borne in the leaf axils towards the tips of the upright stems, and are followed by long flattened pods (green ripening to brown).

👑 Vervaine *Phyla nodiflora*

Vervenn | Height to 15cm; stem length to 1m | ?Introduced
Found: granitics | corallines

A short herb, only a few centimetres tall, with creeping stems, rooting at the nodes, and small flower heads each less than 1cm in height, with many tiny pink flowers. It occurs in damp places, grassland and lawns, especially close to sea level, on granitic and coralline islands.

👑 **Rat's Tails** *Stachytarpheta urticifolia*

Zepi Ble | Height to 1.5m | Introduced

Found: granitics | corallines | Aldabra; Astove

A widespread introduced herb with dark blue flowers carried on long green spikes. Two species of blue-flowered *Stachytarpheta* occur in the granitic and coralline islands; *S. jamaicensis* has pale blue flowers and leaves with shallow marginal serrations, while *S. urticifolia* has darker flowers and the marginal serrations of each leaf are more pronounced.

👑 **Turnera** *Turnera angustifolia*

Koket | Height 1m | Introduced

Found: granitics | corallines | Aldabra

A herb with long, roughly hairy leaves that was introduced as an ornamental for its large yellow flowers, and is now widespread. The base of the stem sometimes becomes woody.

👑 *Wedelia trilobata*

Height 25cm; stem length to 40cm | Introduced

Found: granitics; Mahé, Praslin, La Digue | corallines; a few hotel islands

An introduced ornamental herb originating in the tropical Americas, recently much-planted for ground cover in gardens and roadside 'beautification' plantings. It has creeping stems bearing simple or three-lobed dark green leaves and bright yellow daisy flowers. In some tropical countries it has become an invasive weed. On Aldabra and Assumption, the similar native species *Melanthera biflora* occurs.

👑 **Crinum Lily** *Crinum* hybrid

Lis | Height to 1.5m | Introduced

Found: granitics; Mahé, Praslin, La Digue | corallines; gardens on some islands

The genus *Crinum* includes a number of ornamental lilies introduced to Seychelles' gardens, some of which have become naturalised. This hybrid is usually seen in gardens. Other *Crinum* species include: *C. asiaticum*, a huge plant with broad leaves from a stout upright stem and football-sized flower heads of white flowers, each with narrow petals; *C. amabile*, with white-pinkish drooping flowers; and *C. angustum*, with large strap-like leaves and erect pink flowers.

👑 Crepe Ginger *Costus speciosus*

Height to 2.5m | Introduced

Found: granitics; Mahé, Praslin, Silhouette, La Digue

Found along roadsides and in light shade from low to mid-altitudes, this herb has red cone-like flowering structures borne at the tips of the leafy stems. Individual flowers are large, white and showy.

👑 Banana *Musa sapientum*

Pye Bannann | Height to 6m | Introduced

Found: granitics | corallines; many inhabited islands

An enormous herb; the tree-like trunk is made up of leaf stems growing from a basal corm. The flower spike is a large downward-pointing structure with purple bracts concealing rows of flowers. There are many varieties of bananas in Seychelles, including small, sweet eating bananas and large green cooking bananas (plantains).

👑 Parrot Flower *Heliconia psittacorum*

Height to 2m | Introduced

Found: granitics; Mahé, Praslin, Silhouette, La Digue

A relative of bananas, with elongate leaves and long-stemmed flower heads consisting of well-spaced orange bracts containing long orange flowers. Several other *Heliconia* species are grown for their ornamental bracts, often yellow and red, which last well as cut flowers. This is one of the most widely grown, occuring in gardens and roadside vegetation.

👑 Giant Arum or Titan Lily *Amorphophallus paeoniifolius*

Soul Mous | Height to 3m | Introduced

Found: granitics; Mahé, Praslin, Silhouette, La Digue

A large terrestrial herb, represented for much of the year by a small group of gigantic leaves held on succulent green mottled stems arising from an underground rhizome (main picture). A purple, foul-smelling flowering body (inset) is produced from the rhizome. Perhaps introduced as a starvation food, the rhizomes can be eaten but must be well prepared beforehand to remove toxins. It can be found in grassy places and waste land on Mahé, Praslin and perhaps other islands, but is not common.

👑 Cat's Whiskers or Bat Plant *Tacca leontopetaloides*

Larourout | Height (flower stem) to 1m+ | Introduced

Found: granitics; Mahé and satellites, Praslin, Silhouette, La Digue, Marianne | corallines; Amirantes (D'Arros)

An unusual herb, usually represented by a single, much-divided leaf. The flower stem, sometimes over 1m tall, bears a cluster of green flowers with long threadlike bracts. Flowers are followed by globular, ribbed green fruit. Like *Amorphophallus*, this plant has a starchy rhizome that can be used as a foodstuff in time of shortage but needs careful preparation to remove toxins.

Bougainvillea *Bougainvillea spectabilis (B. glabra)*
Vilea | Climbing stems to 10m | Introduced

Found: granitics; all inhabited islands | corallines; hotel islands

A spectacular, much-cultivated climbing plant, with spiny stems. The 'flowers' of Bougainvillea are actually coloured bracts (modified leaves) surrounding the small, pale, tubular flowers. The bracts may be purple, mauve, red, pink, white, or orange. Some forms are double, with dense clusters of bracts. Bougainvillea flowers year-round, but is particularly prominent in the late dry season and early wet season.

Passion Flower *Passiflora edulis*
Frilapasyon | Climbing stems to 10m | Introduced

Found: granitics; Mahé and satellites, Praslin, Silhouette, La Digue, Frégate

The edible passion fruit is produced by this rampant introduced vine, which originated in South America. The plant climbs by means of tendrils, reaching the tops of trees, and has white flowers 8cm across. The spherical fruit are 4–6cm across, and occur in two colour forms; yellow or purple when ripe. A hard, smooth skin encloses sweet pulp and seeds. This species is commonly cultivated and also widespread in woodland.

Rangoon Creeper *Quisqualis indica*
Lalyann Vermiuz | Climbing stems to 15m | Introduced

Found: granitics; Mahé and satellites, Praslin, Silhouette, La Digue, Cousin

A very invasive liana originally from Africa and Asia, but now widespread throughout the tropics where it has been introduced as an ornamental garden plant. The stems have paired opposite leaves and terminal clusters of scented hanging flowers, each of which is made up of an elongate green tube ending in five purple-red 'petals'.

Blue Trumpet Vine *Thunbergia grandiflora*
Climbing stems to 15m | Introduced

Found: granitics; Mahé and satellites, Praslin, La Digue

Blue Trumpet Vine has large pale blue or white trumpet-shaped flowers grouped in hanging racemes, and ovate or pointed toothed leaves up to 20cm long. An abundant and vigorous climber found at low to middle altitudes on the larger granitic islands, where it can carpet hillsides and smother trees and shrubs. Originally introduced from Asia as an ornamental plant, it is now well established along roadsides, on waste ground and in scrubby vegetation.

Merremia peltata
Lalyann d'Argent | Climbing stems to 20m | Introduced
Found: granitics; Mahé, Silhouette

A widespread and abundant introduced liana in lowland and mid-altitude parts of Mahé. Here, it grows vigorously in disturbed places such as waste ground and alongside roads, or on the edge of secondary forest. It is often seen smothering shrubs and even large trees as in this photograph. *Merremia* has large, heart-shaped peltate leaves and clusters of pale yellow morning glory-like flowers.

Copperleaf   *Acalypha wilkesiana*
Akalypha | Height to 4m | Introduced
Found: granitics; Mahé and satellites, Praslin, Silhouette, La Digue | corallines; Bird, Denis, Amirantes

This variable shrub is very common in Seychelles' gardens, where it is cultivated for its decorative foliage. A common variety (*A. w.* 'Marginata') has ovate purple-brown leaves edged with pink; others are all-purple, pink-blotched or streaked, or green with cream variegations. The flowers are insignificant and occur on small green tassels like catkins. *Acalypha wilkesiana* originated in Polynesia but is now widespread in cultivation. The related endemic shrub *A. claoxyloides* occurs on Aldabra and the introduced herb *A. indica* occurs on many granitic and coralline islands.

Pride of Barbados   *Caesalpinia pulcherrima*
Zegret | Height to 4m | Introduced
Found: granitics; Mahé and satellites, Praslin, Silhouette, La Digue | corallines; Bird, Denis, Amirantes (D'Arros)

A common garden shrub with delicate feathery leaves made up of many small leaflets, and open clusters of attractive flowers, each with ruffled petals and protruding yellow/orange stamens and style. The petals may be yellow, orange, or pink, edged in yellow. Dry purple-brown seedpods follow the flowers. Although this can become a large shrub, it is more commonly seen at about 2m tall. It is often used in roadside 'beautification' plantings.

🌳 Hibiscus or Rose of China *Hibiscus species and hybrids*
Ibiskis | Height to 5m | Introduced
Found: granitics; Mahé and satellites, Praslin, Silhouette, La Digue | corallines; Bird, Denis, Amirantes (inhabited islands only)

Hibiscus plants are found in almost every garden. *Hibiscus rosa-sinensis* is a common species with glossy dark-green leaves and bright crimson flowers 10cm across, but *H. schitzopetalus* can also be found; the latter species forms an untidy, leggy bush with small, red, hanging flowers with narrow, divided petals. There are also numerous hybrids of these and other species, with flowers in red, pink, white, or orange shades. Some varieties have variegated leaves or double flowers.

🌳 *Pithecollobium unguis-cati*
Kanpes | Height to 5m | Introduced
Found: granitics; Mahé and satellites, Praslin, Silhouette, La Digue | corallines; Denis, Amirantes (D'Arros, St Joseph)

A dense bushy shrub or small tree, often seen trimmed as a hedge but also established in the wild, for example in coastal woodland on La Digue, and some coralline islands. The stems are spiny and the leaves each have two pairs of rounded leaflets. The flowers (*a*) are small yellow-white pompoms and the fruit are hanging, spiral pods (*b*), which turn reddish before opening to reveal the black seeds, each of which has a red fleshy base (aril).

🌳 Lantana *Lantana camara*
Vye Fiy | Height to 3m | Introduced
Found: granitics; Mahé and satellites, Praslin, Silhouette, La Digue, North | corallines; Denis, Platte, Coëtivy, Amirantes (Desroches, D'Arros, St Joseph, Poivre, Marie-Louise, Alphonse), Farquhar (Providence, Farquhar) | Aldabra; Aldabra

A dense, weedy shrub, with spiny stems and small, rough leaves. The small flowers are carried in rounded flower heads at the tips of stems; each opens pale yellow, turning pink with age. There is also an orange-flowered variety. The fruit are small blue-black berries, which are eaten by birds. Lantana originates in the Antilles and has been introduced around the world as an ornamental plant, becoming a major pest, especially in the dry tropics. In Seychelles, it is widespread in open places at low-mid altitudes on granitic and coralline islands. It can grow in light shade but does not thrive in woodland or shady places.

Wild Tamarind *Leucaena leucocephala*

Kassie | Height to 10m | Introduced

Found: granitics; Mahé and satellites, Praslin, Silhouette, La Digue | corallines; Denis, Platte, Coëtivy, Amirantes (Remire, D'Arros, St Joseph, Marie-Louise), Farquhar (some islands)

An invasive introduced shrub or small tree, occasionally reaching 10m but usually much less. It rapidly spreads to form a dense clump of erect, sparsely branched woody stems, bearing feathery pinnate leaves. The flowers are groups of off-white pompoms, followed by clusters of flattened woody pods. It grows well in full sun or partial shade on waste ground and in former plantations, losing vigour in shade.

Castor Oil Plant *Ricinus communis*

Tantan, Risin | Height to 5m | Introduced

Found: granitics; Mahé and satellites, Praslin, Silhouette, La Digue, Cousin | corallines; Bird, Denis, Coëtivy, Amirantes and Farquhar (Desroches, D'Arros, Marie-Louise, Alphonse) | Aldabra

A short-lived shrub, with large lobed leaves and spiny flower-heads and fruits. The seeds are poisonous to humans, although they are eaten by some birds and yield an oil with medicinal use. It was once cultivated and is now widely naturalised in coastal lowlands.

Papaya or Pawpaw *Carica papaya*

Papaie | Height to 10m | Introduced

Found: granitics; Mahé and satellites, Praslin, Silhouette, La Digue, Cousin | corallines; Bird, Denis, Amirantes (most islands) | Aldabra; Aldabra

Introduced for its large orange fruit, eaten raw when ripe or cooked if picked green. It has successfully invaded natural habitats on coastal plateaux and coralline islands, growing rapidly to exploit gaps in the canopy. Individuals are either male or female; female trees have few, large flowers carried on the main stem, and bear the fruit. Male plants have long trailing sprays of smaller flowers.

Frangipani *Plumeria rubra*

Franzipann | Height to 6m | Introduced

Found: granitics; almost all inhabited islands | corallines; Bird, Denis, Amirantes (some inhabited islands)

A small tree with thick twigs and milky sap, native to Central America but now widespread in the tropics. The highly scented flowers may be pink, yellow, or off-white. A related species, *P. obtusa*, makes a larger tree with glossy, blunt-tipped leaves and larger flowers which are always white with a yellow throat.

Flamboyant Tree *Delonix regia*
Flambwayan | Height to 10m | Introduced

Found: granitics; almost all inhabited islands | corallines; Denis, Amirantes (rare)

A beautiful tree originally endemic to Madagascar, where wild populations are now under threat due to deforestation. As an ornamental tree, it has been planted throughout the tropics. It is unmistakable in flower, when it is smothered in bright red or orange flowers. Even out of flower, the tree is quite distinctive, with its flat-topped form, large, very delicate pinnate leaves – almost fernlike in appearance – and broad, hanging, woody seedpods.

Banyan *Ficus benghalensis*
Miltipiyan | Height to 15m | Introduced

Found: granitics; Mahé, Praslin, Silhouette, La Digue, Frégate | corallines; Denis, Coëtivy, Amirantes (D'Arros), Farquhar (Farquhar)

A large, spreading tree with many aerial roots that can descend to the ground and may develop into thick buttresses. The leaves are relatively broad and leathery, and the tree bears red fruit, loved by Blue Pigeons. Many fine trees can be seen on Frégate and Denis islands. A useful shade tree, it has been widely planted.

Breadfruit *Artocarpus altilis*
Friapen | Height to 15m | Introduced

Found: granitics; Mahé, Praslin, Silhouette, La Digue, Frégate | corallines; Denis, Amirantes (D'Arros)

A common garden tree. Breadfruit leaves are large, lobed and dark glossy green, and the large rounded fruits are green, ripening to yellow. There are two main varieties in Seychelles; in the common form, the fruits are harvested green and boiled, baked, or fried as chips. The fruits are sterile, having no seed, and this form can only be propagated vegetatively. The fruit are a useful starchy staple food. A second, rather uncommon form called breadnut has much bigger, less deeply lobed leaves and smaller fruits full of seeds, which are cooked and eaten. In mid-high-altitude forests, the related Jackfruit *A. heterophyllus* is common; it has huge (to 50cm long) warty yellow fruit held on the main stems.

Glacis and Scrub

Glacis is open, rocky habitat found on the granitic islands at all elevations. Even at low altitudes, it is home to a range of native and endemic species.

Where red-earth soils cover the underlying granite, denser vegetation can form. Hill slopes with eroded, nutrient-poor soils support scrub, often made up of native plants, often with the Bracken Fern (*see* Ferns section). Scrub vegetation covers large areas in the south of Mahé, Praslin and Curieuse. It is also the dominant vegetation type of Aldabra, where it includes a mixture of species shared with the granitic islands and some Aldabra endemics.

🌱 Mauritius Hemp or Century Plant *Furcraea foetida*

Lalwa | Leaves to 1m+, Flower Stem to 5m | Introduced
Found: granitics; most large and medium islands | corallines; Denis

A large succulent herb, with a rosette of stiff leaves, each with a terminal spine and sometimes red marginal spines. Once grown for fibre, it is now widely naturalised in open areas. The plant grows for many years before putting all its energy into a single flowering event, after which it dies. The tree-like flowering stem bears many flowers and small plantlets (bulbils). The similar Sisal *Agave sisalana* is also widespread.

🌱 *Dianella ensifolia*

Mangasave | Height to 1.5m | ?Introduced
Found: granitics; Mahé and satellites

A clump-forming herb, with upright stems bearing strap-like leaves. The small blue flowers are carried on short branches from the wiry flower stem, and are followed by porcelain-blue berries 1.5cm across. A species of restricted distribution, but abundant where it does occur, especially on Mahé and Thérèse.

🌱 Pineapple *Ananas comosus*

Zannannan | Height to 90cm | Introduced
Found: granitics; most large and medium islands

A crop plant originating in South America, the pineapple forms a rosette of tough spiny leaves. A small-fruited variety, the 'mosquito pineapple', is abundant in open rocky places. Larger-fruited cultivars are grown here, but many of the Pineapples consumed in local hotels are imported.

🌱 Aldabra Lily *Lomatophyllum aldabraense*

Zannan Mowo | Height to 2m | Endemic
Found: Aldabra; Aldabra, Assumption, Astove

Found only on Aldabra, this endemic shrubby herb forms rosettes of long, pointed succulent leaves. Tall spikes of tubular orange flowers are produced, mainly in the late wet season or early dry season. The flowers are followed by purple-red berries which are eaten by Blue Pigeons and bulbuls.

♕ *Cynorkis* sp.

Orkid | Height to 25cm | Native/Endemic
Found: granitics; Mahé, Praslin, Silhouette, Curieuse

 A common terrestrial orchid, found growing on red-earth soils in open grassy places and dappled shade. One or two long, strap-like, glossy leaves occur at ground level and a narrow, leafless flower stem to 25cm tall bears a few small cream and pink flowers.

♕ Pigeon Orchid *Dendrobium crumenatum*

Orkid | Height to 40cm | Introduced
Found: granitics; Mahé

 An epiphytic orchid that occurs from sea level to high altitudes, but is probably most abundant growing on trees and rocks at mid-altitudes. The plant has upright, swollen stems (pseudobulbs) and narrow, leathery leaves each to 7cm long. Flower stems bear the small white flowers, which are said to resemble birds in flight, hence the English name. It occurs on Mahé and its satellite islands.

♕ Tropicbird Orchid *Angraecum eburneum*

Fler Payanke | Height to 1.5m | Native
Found: granitics; Mahé, Silhouette, Praslin | Aldabra; Aldabra

 The national flower of Seychelles, this orchid has beautiful large flowers up to 6cm wide, with white and green petals and sepals. Each flower is backed by a slender green spur to 15cm long (to 7cm in the Aldabra subspecies); this, and the white 'wings' (sepals) give the plant its common name. The plant grows in open rocky places, such as higher altitude glacis; in woodland; or, on Aldabra, as an epiphyte on mangroves. Plants in accessible places are often removed (illegally) for cultivation in private gardens. Two different subspecies occur, one on the granitic islands and one on Aldabra.

♕ Wild Vanilla *Vanilla phalaenopsis*

Lavannir Maron | Stems to 3m | Endemic
Found: granitics; Mahé and satellites, Praslin, Silhouette, Félicité

 This relative of the cultivated vanilla is a climbing and scrambling liana with thick, succulent stems devoid of leaves. It can survive in open, dry places and is found on many of the islands in the granitic group. The beautiful white flowers, each up to 8cm across, are unmistakable and are followed by cylindrical fruits up to 15cm long.

Sarcostemma viminale

Lalyann Sans Fey | Stems to 3m | Native

Found: granitics; most large and medium islands | Aldabra; Aldabra, Assumption, Astove, Cosmoledo

A climbing or scrambling plant composed of many narrow, leafless stems. Photosynthesis is carried out by the succulent green stems, a strategy to limit water loss in exposed and dry areas such as glacis. The flowers are small and cream-yellow, borne in dense clusters at the tips of branches. The stems are narrow and mid-green, paler and thinner than those of wild vanilla.

Pitcher Plant or Monkey Cups   *Nepenthes pervillei*

Lalyann Potao | Stems to 5m | Endemic

Found: granitics; Mahé, Silhouette

An endemic liana of Mahé, Silhouette and Praslin, found in woodland, scrub and open areas on red-earth soils, often in association with bracken fern, and on glacis. In more sheltered places, the stems reach several metres in length and climb in shrubs and trees using tendrils (from leaf tips) for support. Many leaves bear terminal 'pitchers', which are insect traps that provide the plant with additional nutrients. The pitchers may be up to 20cm long – although very young plants bear tiny pitchers a fraction of this size – and are deep, lidded containers with nectar-producing organs around the lip to attract ants and other invertebrates. The smooth inner surfaces of the pitcher do not provide a good grip and many insects slip and fall into the liquid in the lower pitcher, where they drown. Cells lining the pitcher produce digestive chemicals and absorb nutrients from the liquid. The lid of the pitcher prevents it filling with rainwater. *Nepenthes* is primarily an Asian genus; this is one of the westernmost outlying species.

Canthium   *Canthium bibracteatum*

Bwa Dir | Height to 7m | Native

Found: granitics; most islands | Aldabra; Aldabra

An upright shrub or small tree bearing opposite, lanceolate leaves. The midrib of each leaf is often red-maroon in colour, sometimes green as illustrated. The flowers are insignificant and are followed by small spherical fruit, brown when ripe. These are attractive to native fruit-feeding birds such as the Blue Pigeon. Canthium wood is very durable and sharpened stakes, driven into the ground, are used to husk coconuts. Two other endemic species of *Canthium* occur on the granitic islands.

Cocoplum *Chrysobalanus icaco*

Prin-d-frans | Height 50cm–3m (exceptionally 4–5m) | Introduced
Found: granitics; most islands

This invasive scrambling shrub originated in South America and has been widely planted on the granitic islands for erosion control, and is now widespread in scrub and woodland. In open places, it can form a dense ground cover of matted stems from 50cm to 3m. Very rarely, individual plants form upright trees 4–5m high. The arching stems bear tough, shiny round leaves and spherical fruit. The fruit are wrinkled and green when young but become pink (or white) and smooth when ripe. Although edible, they are rather tasteless with a tough skin and soft, wet white flesh around a single large ridged seed.

Dragon Tree *Dracaena reflexa*

Bwa Sandel | Height to 5m | Native
Found: granitics; most islands | Aldabra; Aldabra, Assumption

A rather palm-like shrub with upright stems, the tip of each stem bearing clusters of elongate leaves. The individual flowers are small and whitish, but they are borne en masse on branched hanging inflorescences. The fruit is a spherical orange berry 1cm across. The plant is used medicinally in Seychelles. It is found in scrub, woodland and open places throughout the granitic islands and on Aldabra and Assumption. Several related species, often with colourful foliage, occur in gardens.

Memecylon eleagni

Bwa Kalou | Height to 3m (exceptionally to 8m) | Endemic
Found: granitics; Mahé and satellites, Praslin, Silhouette, Curieuse

A shrub to 3m tall, occasionally growing as a tree to 8m, found in dry scrub and glacis from sea level to mid-altitudes. It is densely bushy and upright, with ovoid-rounded leathery leaves each 2–5cm long. The flowers are small, up to 1cm across, white-petalled, and are followed by small spherical blue-black fruits to 1cm in diameter.

Paragenipa wrightii

Kafe Maron Gran Fey | Height to 6m (usually less) | Endemic
Found: granitics; Mahé and satellites, Praslin, Round Island, Silhouette, Curieuse

An upright shrub, found in dry scrub and glacis from sea level to mid-altitudes. The leathery elongate leaves reach 15cm long, and are dark green, often with a reddish tinge. The small flowers have five white petals fused into a short tube and are carried singly or in small groups. The fruit are elongate-ovoid in shape, to 2cm long and bright red in colour. The leaf and fruit resemble those of coffee, giving the plant its Creole name.

Pemphis *Pemphis acidula*

Bwa Daman | Height to 5m | Native
Found: corallines; Amirantes (St Joseph) | Aldabra

A large, salt-tolerant shrub, growing on land or in the margins of fresh, brackish or salt water. It forms dense, impenetrable thickets of scratchy twigs bearing small leaves and small, white, six-petalled flowers (*a*). It is abundant on Aldabra and some of the Amirantes, but absent from the granitics and the northern coralline islands of Bird and Denis.

Sideroxylon inerme

Bwa Zak | Height to 5m | Native
Found: Aldabra

A shrub with leathery rounded leaves and small greenish flowers carried on the stems. The fruit are small and globose, black when mature, and are eaten by Blue Pigeons. It is common on Aldabra, especially on the jagged limestone 'champignon', and neighbouring islands.

Alstonia or Scholar Tree *Alstonia macrophylla*

Bwa Zonn | Height to 15m | Introduced
Found: granitics; most islands

A recently introduced species that has quickly become an invasive weed-tree in the granitic islands. It is identified by its gaunt pale stems and whorls of branches bearing long, pale green leaves. Panicles of small flowers are followed by clusters of elongate, down-hanging narrow pods becoming brown when ripe. This tree is abundant in very open, dry locations including glacis and eroded red-earth soils on most islands.

Jellyfish Tree *Medusagyne oppositifolia*

Bwa Mediz | Height to 8m | Endemic
Found: granitics; Mahé

This extraordinary small tree was presumed extinct in the 1960s before being rediscovered in 1970. Today, over 40 scattered individuals remain on Mahé, mainly in exposed rocky situations between 150-500m. The species has been placed in its own family, the Medusagynaceae, although some authorities place it in the tea family Theaceae. Like the tea plant, it has glossy evergreen leaves – often with a few bright red leaves scattered on the tree – and white flowers. Clusters of flowers are followed by groups of small ovoid fruits, which ripen and dry out to release seed, becoming red-brown and opening like tiny parasols 1-1.5cm across. Unlike most endemic trees, the seeds of the Jellyfish Tree are distributed by the wind; an unusual strategy for island plants, as it can result in a high degree of seed wastage.

Mid-altitude Forests and Forestry Plantations

At mid-altitudes on the granitic islands, forests are dominated by introduced crop trees, particularly Cinnamon and Albizzia, also rubber, Oil Palm, cloves, Butternut and a variety of fruit trees. The lower storey of such forests usually supports a sparse growth of ferns and introduced herbs, except at clearings and roadsides where additional light reaches the ground and encourages the growth of large ferns like *Angiopteris*, lianas, *Dieffenbachia*, and many introduced shrubs.

There are areas of plantation on the larger granitic islands of Mahé and Praslin. Timber plantations are usually made up of a single species, either Santol or Mahogany; the understorey is usually sparse although some of the endemic palms may survive. At higher mid-altitudes on Mahé, Tea is grown in small patches of former forest land.

☙ Dumb Cane *Dieffenbachia sequine*

Vya Tang | Height to 1.5m | Introduced
Found: granitics; Mahé, Praslin, Silhouette, La Digue

An attractive, large-leafed herb first introduced as a garden ornamental and now widely distributed in the wild, particularly in woodland at mid-altitudes on Mahé and Praslin. The leaves are usually splashed with white or cream-coloured variegation. The sap is an irritant.

☙ *Curculigo sechellensis*

Koko Maron | Height to 2m | Endemic
Found: granitics; Mahé, Praslin, Silhouette, Curieuse, Félicité, Thérèse

An upright, large terrestrial herb, resembling a young palm. It is distinguished from the closely related *Hypoxidia* by size and by the leaf stems, which are heavily armed with black thorns. The flowers, which vary in colour from pale cream to bright yellow, are clustered at the base of the plant and are more frequently seen than those of *Hypoxidia*. This plant grows in a range of habitats at middle and higher altitudes, including glacis and scrub, palm forest and mist forest.

☙ *Hypoxidia rhizophylla*

Pti Koko Maron | Height to 50cm | Endemic
Found: granitics; Mahé, Praslin, Silhouette, La Digue, Curieuse, Félicité

A small terrestrial herb with narrow leaves each up to 90cm. Mainly found in mid- to higher-altitude forests, but sometimes in more open, rocky places. The tough, strap-shaped leaves arise from an underground rhizome. Leaves root at the tips, forming new plantlets, and so small colonies can form in suitable locations. The basal, star-shaped flowers are short-lived and rarely seen, and vary in colour from yellow to dark maroon-brown. The similar *H. maheensis* occurs only at high altitudes on Mahé and is larger with broader leaves and pink-brown flowers.

Star of Bethlehem *Hippobroma longiflora*

Lerb Pwazon | Height to 50cm | Introduced
Found: granitics; Mahé, Praslin, Silhouette, La Digue | corallines; Denis, Amirantes
(D'Arros)

A herb with white flowers, each with a long corolla tube (to 10cm) terminating with five splayed 'petals' forming a star shape. Found on waste ground and shaded banks to medium altitudes, mainly on granitic islands but also on some coralline islands. The sap is white and poisonous.

Golden Pothos, Devil's Ivy or 'Philodendron' *Epipremnum aureum*

Philodendron | Stems to 15m | Introduced
Found: granitics; Mahé, Praslin, Silhouette, La Digue

An invasive liana, introduced as an ornamental plant and now abundant in mid-altitude forest, especially on Mahé and Praslin, and also still widely grown in gardens. It has succulent yellow or green climbing stems and large, gold-splashed leaves. Detached pieces of stem root readily.

Vanilla *Vanilla planifolia*

Lavannir | Stems to 30m | Introduced
Found: granitics; Mahé, Praslin, Curieuse, Silhouette, La Digue | corallines; Denis,
Amirantes (D'Arros)

This vine was once an important feature of the island economy, grown on many of the granitic and coralline islands. Small plantations were made where the vines were grown up support trees, and a few examples may still be seen on Mahé and La Digue. However, production is uneconomic and has essentially ceased in Seychelles. Vanilla plants have survived and entered natural habitats, reproducing vegetatively with sections of stem rooting once detached from the plant. They can be distinguished from the endemic Vanilla by the presence of ovoid leaves arranged alternately on the stem. Flowers are rare, and are less showy than those of the endemic Vanilla. There is no natural pollinator in Seychelles, so seed-pods do not form except where the flowers are pollinated by humans.

Tea Plant *Camellia sinensis*

Dite | Height to 10m | Introduced
Found: granitics; Mahé, Praslin

A large shrub, potentially reaching several metres in height but, in plantations, kept very short by regular clipping. Tea production in Seychelles started in 1966, and there are now small patches of plantation all along the higher part of the Sans Souci road to Morne Blanc, Mahé. The Tea Plant seeds itself in forest, where it can form dense stands. It has small white flowers (3cm across) with fleshy petals and a central boss of gold stamens, followed by a three-chambered woody fruit.

Albizzia *Paraserianthes falcataria*

Albizia | Height to 35m | Introduced

Found: granitics; Mahé, Praslin, Silhouette, La Digue, Curieuse, Félicité, Frégate, North

Albizzia, which originates in South-East Asia, was introduced in Seychelles after the 1930s, probably for its low-quality timber. It grows exceptionally quickly, soon forming a tall, flat-topped tree; in Java, it can reach 35m in ten years. It is especially abundant at mid-high altitudes where it often grows along the banks of seasonal streams and as an 'emergent' tree above the canopy of Cinnamon forest. The fernlike leaves cast a light shade. At certain times of year, Albizzia trees flower en masse, producing pompoms of white-yellow scented flower that give off a sweet scent. Flowers are followed by short, erect seedpods that snap open while still on the tree to disperse small brown bean-like seeds. Albizzia is an invasive species that has been blamed for drought and excluding native trees.

Sandragon *Pterocarpus indicus*

Sandragon | Height to 30m | Introduced

Found: granitics; Mahé, Praslin, Silhouette, La Digue, Curieuse, Félicité, Frégate | corallines; Denis

Sandragon is a large tree originating in India, with thick, flaking bark and, in old trees, prominent buttress roots at the base. It is naturally deciduous, losing its pinnate leaves during the dry season. Attractive yellow flowers are borne soon after the new leaves emerge. The name of the tree comes from its red sap ('dragon's blood'), which oozes from damaged stems. Traditionally planted at the boundary of properties and as a shade tree, found for example at the Mission site on Mahé (pictured). In recent years, a fungal disease has damaged many trees, causing foliage loss, and the death of whole trees.

Tabebuia pallida

Kalis Dipap | Height to 15m | Introduced

Found: granitics; almost all islands | corallines; Denis, Amirantes (D'Arros) | Aldabra; Astove

A small-medium tree, with glossy palmate leaves, each bearing 3-5 leaflets. Leaflets are up to 10cm long with rather rounded tips. The flowers are pale pink trumpets up to 6cm long, and are followed by long narrow hanging seedpods. Seeds are flattened and papery. This species is found on many islands, granitic and coralline, and survives in a variety of habitats from the seashore to the mountains.

Cinnamon *Cinnamomum verum*
Kanel | Height to 15m | Introduced
Found: granitics; almost all islands

Cinnamon was one of the earliest of the economic plants to be introduced to the fledgling colony of Seychelles, forming part of a spice garden established in 1772 at Anse Royale, Mahé. From here it made its way into the surrounding vegetation, distributed by fruit-eating birds, and it proved highly successful in its new environment. However, it was not seriously exploited by commerce until the early years of the 20th century, when cinnamon leaf oil was produced in distilleries dotted around the hills of Mahé. In order to produce leaf oil, Cinnamon stems were cropped on a 10–15-year cycle. Distilleries also needed wood fuel, so forest trees were cut. The cutting of native vegetation, deliberate planting and coppicing of Cinnamon led to an expansion of Cinnamon-dominated vegetation through the hills of Mahé. Export of cinnamon leaf oil declined steadily from about 1950 and there are now no working distilleries left. Cinnamon is still cropped for bark on a modest scale, but the spice does not contribute significantly to Seychelles' economy. Cinnamon is perhaps the granitic Seychelles' most abundant tree. It can be identified by the distinctive venation of the leaf, the leaf's cinnamon smell when crushed, and the tree's red new growth and groups of blue-grey berries.

Butternut Tree *Pentadesma butyracea*
Bwa Ber | Height to 15m | Introduced
Found: granitics; Mahé, Praslin

An introduction from West Africa, where the seeds are crushed to produce oil. It has never been utilised since its introduction in the early years of the 20th century, but has spread widely in mid- and high-altitude forests on Mahé and Praslin. *Pentadesma* has a distinctive growth form: regular whorls of branches emanate from a central trunk; each branch bears long, glossy, dark green leaves. Large, waxy off-white flowers are followed by the unmistakable fruit; matt brown with a rather scaly skin, 20–30cm long and almost as wide. The fruit has yellow (inedible) flesh and is packed with large seeds.

Sandoricum koetjape
Santol | Height to 25m | Introduced
Found: granitics; Mahé, Praslin

A plantation tree with trifoliate leaves and orange, rather furry fruit the size of small tangerines. The fruit are edible; beneath the thick skin, they have large seeds coated in an acidic pulpy flesh that has to be sucked from the seed. The tree is grown for its timber.

High-altitude Forests

The highest altitudes of Mahé and Silhouette act as refuges for communities of some of the most interesting endemic shrubs and trees. At sites such as Congo Rouge, Mahé, endemic trees (particularly *Northea*) dominate, and are laden with epiphytic mosses, ferns and orchids. Endemic palms, tree ferns and screwpines also feature in these habitats. In other places such as crests of hills and ridges, a more open, shrubby vegetation forms, again dominated by endemics. The shrubs and trees here support mosses and branching lichens such as *Usnea*. Introduced invasive plant species in higher altitude forests include the ubiquitous Cinnamon, Strawberry Guava and a relatively recent arrival, *Clidemia*.

♛ Seychelles Begonia *Begonia seychellensis*

Lozey Maron | Height to 1.5m | Endemic
Found: granitics; Mahé, Silhouette

An endemic herb, with upright stems bearing attractive leaves, usually dark green with purple-red undersides but sometimes uniform apple green. The flowers are small and pink or white, and the fruit orange-red. It occurs in mid- to high-altitude forests on Mahé and Silhouette.

♛ Busy Lizzie or Wild Balsam *Impatiens gordonii*

Belzamin Sovaz | Height to 1m | Endemic
Found: granitics; Mahé, Silhouette

A tall terrestrial herb. The large white flowers are flat with a curved spur behind. This attractive endemic plant occurs in higher altitude forests on Silhouette, and on Mahé, where it is very rare.

♛ *Malaxis seychellarum*

Orkid | Height to 30cm | Endemic
Found: granitics; Mahé, Silhouette

An abundant ground orchid on Mahé and Silhouette, especially at higher altitudes. It grows in moss on rocks and trees, and on the ground. The tiny flowers, held in an erect spike, are vivid green or purple in colour.

♛ *Bulbophyllum* sp.

Height to 5cm | Native
Found: granitics; Mahé, Silhouette

A tiny epiphytic orchid, found in high-altitude forest and scrub, where it grows on the bark of trees. A narrow creeping rhizome connects small, round pseudobulbs, each of which produces a single narrow leaf. The flowers are white.

🐦 *Polystachya bicolor*

Height to 10cm | Native
Found: granitics; Mahé, Silhouette
A small epiphytic orchid with tiny pink-purple flowers.

🍄 *Aphloia theiformis*

Bwa Merl | Height to 10m | Native
Found: granitics; Mahé, Praslin, Silhouette

A shrub or small tree that occurs from low altitudes to high mountains, in open places, woodland and scrub. Most easily recognised when in fruit, when the twigs bear many white berries each 1cm across. These are eaten and the seed dispersed by fruit-eating birds, including the Seychelles Bulbul (*Merl* in Creole).

🍄 Koster's Curse *Clidemia hirta*

Faux Watouk | Height to 2m | Introduced
Found: granitics; Mahé, Silhouette

This recently introduced shrub, originating in South America, is abundant in parts of Silhouette and appears poised to spread rapidly on Mahé. It can be identified by its hairy, rather nettle-like leaves with prominent regular venation, and small blue-purple fruits, also sparsely hairy. The flowers are small and white. It can come to dominate large areas of forest, especially in clearings where light penetrates the canopy, but is less of a problem in deep shade.

🐦 *Gynura sechellensis*

Zakobe | Height to 2m | Endemic
Found: granitics; Mahé, Silhouette

A shrubby herb found at mid- to high-altitudes in open scrubby vegetation or woodland. The small orange flower heads, resembling those of groundsel, are followed by fluffy seed heads.

🍄 *Gastonia crassa*

Bwa Bannan | Height to 10m | Endemic
Found: granitics; Mahé, Praslin, Silhouette, La Digue, Félicité

A shrub or small tree that grows in woodland and on open mountaintops from around 400m on Mahé (lower on smaller islands). It has glossy pinnate leaves and upright, branching umbels of flowers, which are followed by dark blue-black berries. Two other species of *Gastonia* are endemic to the granitic Seychelles: *G. lionetii* and *G. sechellarum*.

Fungi

A variety of small fungi are found in high-altitude forests, including brightly-coloured species such as that shown.

Chinese or Strawberry Guava *Psidium cattleianum*
Goyave Desin | Height to 7m | Introduced
Found: granitics; Mahé and satellites, Praslin, Silhouette, La Digue, Frégate,
North, Marianne

A common invasive species, introduced originally for its fruit, which are small guavas, red when ripe and particularly tasty. On the granitic islands, its seeds were dispersed in natural habitats by birds. It now occurs into the highest forest, especially in mountain mist forest where it can survive shade and grows into thin-stemmed treelets, sometimes with adventitious roots growing from the stems. It also grows strongly in open, exposed places where the glossy ovate leaves may appear bluish green. The bark is red and peels in flakes or strips. The Common Guava *P. guajava* is more frequent at low altitudes, on the coastal plain and in cultivated areas. It has elongate, roughly hairy leaves and larger fruit.

Wild Bilimbi *Colea seychellarum*
Bilenbi Maron | Height to 10m | Endemic
Found: granitics; Mahé, Praslin, Silhouette

 A small tree or shrub, with pinnate leaves and attractive pale yellow tubular flowers held in an inflorescence growing directly from the woody trunk or branches. The fruits are green and cylindrical. This species usually occurs in moist forest or scrub at the highest altitudes.

Dillenia *Dillenia ferruginea*
Bwa Rouz | Height to 20m | Endemic
Found: granitics; Mahé, Praslin, Silhouette, Curieuse

 An endemic tree of open, dry red-earth slopes and damp woodland at middle and high altitudes, and recognisable by its thick, ridged leaves, almost always peppered with holes produced by herbivorous *Cratopus* weevils. The flowers are white, and develop into a small segmented orange fleshy fruit surrounded by dry brown sepals.

Northea *Northea hornei*
Kapisen | Height to 20m | Endemic
Found: granitics; Mahé, Praslin, Silhouette, Curieuse, Félicité

 A tall tree, sometimes just a large shrub, found in mid-altitude and highland forests of Mahé, Silhouette and Praslin. A few individuals occur at lower altitudes and in open habitats on Curieuse and Félicité. The distinctive foliage colour makes it easily recognisable, even from a distance; the upperside of leaves is grey-green and the underside usually velvety red-brown. Closer up, the plants have thick, stumpy twigs and large spherical fruits (10cm across), each enclosing a single huge hard seed. The seed is glossy brown with a rough scar, said to resemble the hooded head of a Capuchin monk, giving the tree its Creole name.

Palms

The palms of Seychelles include six species endemic to the granitic islands, as well as one widespread native species (the Coconut) and a large number of introduced species, most restricted to gardens. The endemic palms are found on open glacis, scrub and woodland habitats on the granitic islands. In places at mid-altitude (as at La Reserve, Mahé, and much of Praslin), native palm forest occurs, dominated by the palms and *Pandanus*. The most famous palm forest is at Vallée de Mai on Praslin, where the Coco de Mer is the dominant species.

 ### Oil Palm *Elaeis guineensis*
Height to 15m | Introduced
Found: granitics; Mahé, Praslin, Frégate

 After Coconut, this is probably the most abundant palm species on Mahé, occurring in woodland and garden habitats from sea level to mid-altitudes. This palm has a dense crown of feather-shaped leaves, each 3–5m long with a green or yellowish central stem. In the leaf bases of the crown, oil palms bear large clusters of purple-black or red fruit; these are the source of palm oil, commonly used in food products. Oil can also be extracted from the seed and it is this 'palm kernel oil' that is used in soap-making.

 ### Raffia Palm *Raphia farinifera*
Rafya | Height to 20m | Introduced
Found: granitics; Mahé, Praslin, Silhouette, La Digue

 This huge feather palm has the longest leaves in the plant kingdom; they may be 18m long and are blue-green, with a central yellow or orange leaf stem. This leaf stem, cut thinly, is used to make traditional blinds. The plant is also the source of raffia fibre. Each plant only flowers once, putting all its energy into the production of long stems of glossy, scaly red-brown fruits and thousands of seeds, before dying. It usually occurs in wet places, from sea level to high-altitude forest.

 ### Coconut *Cocos nucifera*
Pye Koko | Height to 35m | Native
Found: granitics | corallines | Aldabra

 This palm is ubiquitous in Seychelles, partly due to extensive planting as a crop in the 19th and early 20th centuries. Coconut flesh was dried by the sun or in ovens called calorifiers prior to export as copra. The coastal plateau was the prime site for plantations, but Coconuts were planted to mid-altitudes, and some small islands were completely cleared of native vegetation for plantation. Coconuts can tolerate quite saline ground water and thrive on coral islands. The seed is surrounded by a buoyant husk and remains viable for one month, allowing the plant to island-hop.

Palmiste or Millionaire's Salad *Deckenia nobilis*

Palmis | Height to 35m | Endemic

Found: granitics; Mahé, Praslin, Silhouette, La Digue, Curieuse, Félicité, Thérèse, Conception

A statuesque endemic palm of dry glacis and native forest at all altitudes. As a mature plant, it can be identified by the feathery divided leaves and long bare crownshaft, a cylinder of green leaf bases at the top of the trunk. Young plants have divided leaves and yellow spines on the leaf stems and trunk (*see* photograph). The pendulous flowering bodies of this palm are protected as they develop by a spiny sheath, which drops to the ground as the inflorescence matures. This species was historically harvested for the growing tip, shredded and eaten as millionaire's salad. Because (like most palms) it cannot branch, removal of the growing point kills the whole plant. Although the palm is now protected by law, some illegal harvesting still takes place, but most 'palmiste salad' on hotel menus is made from the growing tip of Coconuts.

Coco de Mer or Double Coconut *Lodoicea maldivica*

Koko-d-mer | Height to 35m (male, female less) | Endemic

Found: granitics; Praslin, Curieuse (in wild; widely planted elsewhere)

In the wild, this impressive palm is confined to the islands of Praslin and Curieuse, although there are good numbers of plants in the botanical gardens and some private gardens on Mahé, and small populations on Silhouette and Félicité. It can be seen at its best in the Vallée de Mai and Fond Ferdinand on Praslin. It is the only native fan palm of Seychelles. The leaves of young plants are among the largest in the vegetable kingdom, being up to 10m long. As the plant matures, it develops a trunk up to 35m tall (a), less in the case of female plants. Plants are either male – bearing enormous catkins (b) when mature – or female – bearing the flowers, the largest of any palm, followed by the fruit. Mature female plants (c) carry large numbers of fruit at different stages of development; each fruit may take up to seven years to mature on the plant before falling to the ground (d). The fruit consists of a thin green or brown husk enclosing the huge, bilobed seed, weighing up to 18kg and the largest seed in the world. Every stage of the palm's lifecycle is slow; once the fruit has fallen, months pass before the husk disintegrates and the seed may take two years to germinate. It takes at least 25 years for the palm to reach sexual maturity. The Coco de Mer dominates forest on parts of Praslin and supports a range of animal species; geckos, bees, flies and slugs feed on the pollen of the male plant. The leaf bases of the palm accumulate leaf litter and support unique invertebrate communities. On the higher slopes of Praslin and on Curieuse, Coco de Mer is found in drier, more open vegetation where it appears capable of surviving erosion and fire.

Nephrosperma vanhoutteanum
Latannyen Milpat | Height to 14m | Endemic
Found: granitics; Mahé, Praslin, Silhouette, Curieuse, St Anne, Thérèse, Frégate (introduced)

A palm lacking the well-developed crownshaft of the Palmiste. Mature plants may reach 14m in favourable conditions, but are usually much shorter. This palm is found at all altitudes and in rocky, open locations as well as tall forest. Young plants generally have reddish leaf stems bearing black spines.

Thief Palm *Phoenicophorium borsigianum*
Latannyen Fey | Height to 15m | Endemic
Found: granitics; Mahé, Praslin, Silhouette, La Digue, Curieuse, St Anne, Frégate, Thérèse, Conception

The new leaves of this palm emerge entire but, with time, they often become shredded by the wind. This is perhaps the commonest of the endemic palms, occurring in dry exposed places as well as in mid- and high-altitude forests, where dense growth of seedlings can occur beneath Cinnamon. The young plants can be identified by the undivided leaves, often with an orange border, and orange leaf stems armed with black spines. The leaves of this species are traditionally used as a thatching material, in demand once more for hotel projects.

Roscheria melanochaetes
Latannyen Oban | Height to 8m | Endemic
Found: granitics; Mahé, Praslin, Silhouette

A small palm, with irregular, broad, blunt-tipped leaflets. Emerging leaves are usually red, maturing to dark green and up to 2.5m long. The stem is armed with black spines. This species is generally restricted to damp, high-altitude forest, although it occurs at the Vallée de Mai, it is rare there.

Stilt Palm *Vershaffeltia splendida*
Latannyen Lat | Height to 30m | Endemic
Found: granitics; Mahé, Praslin, Silhouette

An endemic palm with entire, orbicular leaves. (The rounded leaf shape is particularly noticeable in young plants when the leaf stems have scattered black spines.) In exposed places, the mature leaves are shredded by the wind. Older plants develop a cone of stilt roots at the base of the stem (*see* photograph). It is found in mid- and high-altitude forest, particularly in damp valleys.

Screwpines: Genus *Pandanus*

The screwpines are shrubby or treelike plants with long, spirally arranged spiny leaves. Many species have aerial or stilt roots. The fruiting bodies are large, cone-like structures made up of many large segments called drupes.

Useful Pandanus *Pandanus utilis*

Vakwa Sak | Height to 10m | Introduced

Found: granitics; Mahé, Praslin, Silhouette, La Digue, Félicité, Marianne

A small, gaunt screwpine with spiral blue-green leaves, round fruiting bodies and aerial roots towards the base of the trunk. The dried leaves are used for weaving, for example making woven bags.

Pandanus tectorius

Vakwa | Height to 8m | Native

Found: Aldabra; Aldabra

One of two *Pandanus* species found on Aldabra. The hanging fruit are ovoid like those of *P. balfourii*, but are made up of fewer, larger segments, are yellow when ripe and are eaten and dispersed by tortoises.

Pandanus balfourii

Vakwa Bor-d-mer | Height to 7m | Endemic

Found: granitics

The most widespread endemic *Pandanus* of the central Seychelles, with fruiting bodies to 25cm long (pictured) made up of many segments, bright orange when ripe. Some plants have aerial roots.

Horne's Pandanus *Pandanus hornei*

Vakwa Parasol | Height to 20m | Endemic

Found: granitics; Mahé, Praslin, Silhouette, Curieuse

A screwpine with a basal cone of aerial roots and a tall trunk crowned by a parasol of foliage. Grows from sea level (where rare) to high altitudes, usually in damp places such as along stream banks. Fruiting bodies are enormous spherical clusters of drupes.

Pandanus multispicatus

Vakwa-d-montanny, Vakwa Milpat | Height to 3m | Endemic

Found: granitics; Mahé, Praslin, Silhouette, Curieuse, Félicité, Frégate

A small, bushy endemic screwpine with narrow, spiny leaves. The fruiting body is upright and is made up of many tiny drupes, yellowish when ripe. Occurs in scrub and open glacis.

Seychelles Pandanus *Pandanus sechellarum*

Vakwa Maron | Height to 15m | Endemic

Found: granitics; Mahé, Praslin, Silhouette, La Digue

This large endemic screwpine has stout, widely spaced aerial roots. The spherical fruiting bodies are as large as a football. Found in exposed places on cliffs and glacis, and in moist forests.

Grasses and Sedges

Grasses and sedges share the linear, 'grassy' leaf shape and small flowers lacking petals, usually grouped in a terminal inflorescence. Over 100 grass species occur in Seychelles, occurring in almost all habitats. One species is endemic to the granitic islands (*Garnotia sechellensis*, restricted to high-altitude forests and scrub) and six are endemic to the raised coralline islands; five of these are restricted to short grassland on Aldabra maintained by tortoise grazing ('tortoise turf'). There are at least 46 sedge species in Seychelles, three of which are endemic to the granitics and two endemic to the Aldabra group.

Bambusa vulgaris

Bambou, Bambou Zonn | Height to 5m+ | Introduced

Found: granitics; most islands | corallines; Amirantes (D'Arros) | Aldabra; Aldabra

The most widespread bamboo of Seychelles, found on most islands that have had human settlement, often forming large clumps. It occurs in two forms, one with golden yellow stems with occasional green stripes (var. *aureo-variegata*), the other with uniform green stems. The larger, less commonly seen species *Dendrocalamus giganteus* reaches 15m tall.

Lemon Grass   *Cymbopogon* spp.

Sitronel | Height to 1.5m+ | Introduced

Found: granitics; all inhabited islands | corallines; all inhabited islands | Aldabra; Aldabra

A tall grass, with flowering stems 1.5m or more high. Several species occur in cultivation or naturalised, for example along roadsides at mid-altitudes on Mahé. All species form dense clumps of long leaves and bear tall arching flowering stems. The crushed leaves have a strong citronella odour and can be used to make tea.

Guinea Grass   *Panicum maximum*

Fatak | Height to 2.5m | Introduced

Found: granitics | corallines; Bird, Denis, Amirantes (D'Arros, Poivre), Farquhar group | Aldabra

A tall grass, formerly much cultivated and widespread on granitic and coralline islands. Used as a fodder crop, flowering stems were also dried and used to make brooms. Now abundant in grassy waste places and along roadsides.

Dactyloctenium sp.

Lerb Bourik | Height to 20cm | Native

Found: granitics | corallines | Aldabra

A spreading grass of the beach crest and coastal plain on granitic and coralline islands. Flowers are borne in short, fat spikes with up to six spikes held in a whorl at the tip of each flowering stem.

Brachiara umbellata (*Panicum umbellatum*)

Gazon Trel | Height to 20cm (usually much less) | ?Introduced
Found: granitics; most islands | corallines; Denis, Amirantes (D'Arros)

A lawn grass, with short, alternate leaves on stems that may be either creeping or upright, forming dense mats to 20cm thick. Planted to control erosion of hill red-earth soils and as lawns at lower elevations.

Stenotaphrum dimidiatum

Lerb Koko | Height to 40cm | Native
Found: granitics | corallines; Bird, Denis, Coëtivy, Amirantes (Desroches, D'Arros, Marie-Louise, Poivre, Alphonse), Providence, Farquhar

A carpeting, broad-leaved grass often found as ground cover in coconut plantations. The flowering stems are single, flattened spikes with the flowers embedded in one side.

Kyllingia polyphylla

Lerb Zonnyon | Height (flower stems) to 50cm | Native
Found: granitics; almost all islands | corallines; Coëtivy, Amirantes (Rémire, Alphonse) | Aldabra; Aldabra

An abundant sedge of coastal lowlands and hills. Each plant forms a clump of leaves with red basal leaf sheaths and tall leafless flower stems, topped by rounded heads of green flowers, surrounded by a cluster of long green bracts.

Lophoschoenus hornei

Lerb Razwar | Height (leaves) 75cm, (flower stems) 2m | Endemic
Found: granitics; Mahé, Praslin, Silhouette, Curieuse, Félicité, Thérèse

This endemic sedge has tall, arching flower stems bearing red-brown or golden flower-heads. It is found in exposed open glacis at mid-altitudes. The erect rosettes of tough, sharp-edged leaves are bright green or yellowish in colour.

Mapania floribunda

Lerb Razwar | Height to 2m | Endemic
Found: granitics; Mahé, Praslin, Silhouette, Félicité, Marianne, Grand Soeur

A tall, clump-forming endemic sedge with fairly wide, pleated dark green leaves and dense brown flower-heads. Found on many of the granitic islands, usually in mid-altitude forest or dense scrub. The smaller species *M. angustifolium* (to 1m tall, with narrower leaves and sparse flower-heads) occurs on Mahé, Praslin and Silhouette.

Ferns

Ninety or more species of ferns occur in Seychelles, although only a handful occur on the coralline islands and most species are found only on the largest granitic islands of Mahé, Praslin, Silhouette and La Digue.

Bird's Nest Fern *Asplenium nidus*

Lang-d-bef | Height to 1.5m | Native
Found: granitics; Mahé, Praslin, Silhouette, La Digue | corallines; Amirantes (Alphonse)

An epiphytic fern with a shuttlecock of simple, glossy fronds. The Bird's Nest Fern occurs primarily on the larger granitic islands in mid-altitude or higher forests, but is also found on at least one of the coralline islands (Alphonse).

Seychelles Tree Fern *Cyathea sechellarum*

Fanjon | Height to 7m | Endemic
Found: granitics; Mahé, Silhouette

The only Seychelles' fern developing a tall stem, with very large, long (to 2m), much-divided fronds. Most abundant in highest altitude moist forest on Morne Seychellois (Mahé) and Silhouette, but occasional outliers can be found at slightly lower altitudes, for example on Morne Blanc (Mahé).

King, or Giant, Fern *Angiopteris evecta*

Baton Monsennyer | Height to 4m | Native
Found: granitics; Mahé, Praslin, Silhouette

A huge forest fern with giant fronds to 4m long, growing from a woody base. The dark green, glossy fronds are divided into large oblong pinnae. Abundant along road- and stream-sides at mid-altitudes on the large islands.

Bracken or Tangle Fern *Dicranopteris linearis*

Fouzer Koulev | Height to 2.5m | ?Native
Found: granitics; Mahé, Praslin, Silhouette, Thérèse, Pti Soeur

An abundant fern on many of the larger granitic islands. Fronds are much-divided and arise from an underground rhizome. This species thrives in open locations on eroded red-earth soils, where it may form dense thickets over large areas. Beneath the tangled canopy of fronds, dead, dry material accumulates and Bracken Fern can thus be a fire risk.

Microsorum scolopendrium (*Phymatosorus, Phymatodes scolopendria*)

Kapiler | Height to 40cm | Native
Found: granitics | corallines; almost all islands

A widespread, abundant fern, occurring on granitic and coralline islands in most habitats and altitudes. It is often found alongside *Nephrolepis* in coastal coconut plantations. The lobed fronds grow from a creeping rhizome. Fertile fronds have circular clumps of sporangia on the underside, marked by blisters on the upperside of the frond.

Boston, or Course Sword, Fern   *Nephrolepis biserrata*

Fouzer Taba | Height to 2m | Native
Found: granitics | corallines; almost all islands | Aldabra; Aldabra, Assumption

The most widespread fern of Seychelles, growing in most habitats from sea level to mountaintops, on granitic and coralline islands. It is especially abundant close to sea level where it is a dominant part of the ground flora in coconut plantations and woods. The long, arching fronds form dense clumps. The elongate sporangia occur on the underside of the frond.

Filmy Ferns *Trichomanes* spp.

Fronds to 20cm | Native
Found: granitics; Mahé, Praslin, Silhouette, La Digue, Curieuse

The filmy ferns are small to tiny ferns with pellucid fronds only one cell thick. *Trichomanes* species have broad fronds up to 20cm long. *Hymenophyllum* species are generally smaller with narrower fronds up to 10cm long, on creeping wiry black rhizomes. Filmy ferns grow among moss on tree trunks and rocks in damp forest.

Nodding Clubmoss   *Lycopodium cernuum*

Fouzer Maryaz | Height to 1.2m | Native
Found: granitics; Mahé, Praslin, Silhouette, Conception

An unmistakable fern relative, with its stems densely clothed in tiny triangular 'leaves'. Stems are creeping or upright, resembling small Christmas trees with the fruiting bodies carried at the tips of the 'branches'. This species favours eroded red-earth soils at mid-altitudes. It is widely distributed in the tropics.

Spikemoss   *Selaginella fissidentoides*

Lapat Lezar | Height to 10cm | Native
Found: granitics; Mahé, Praslin, Silhouette, Thérèse

A small fern relative that may be mistaken for a moss. The slender creeping stems of Spikemoss grow in moist spots at mid-altitude.

Seagrasses

Seagrasses are higher plants (angiosperms) that have adapted to live a purely marine existence. They grow in shallow seagrass beds on sandy substrates and pieces of the plants are cast up after storms. There are at least eight species in coastal waters of the Seychelles, most widely distributed around the coralline and granitic islands. Three species are shown here: *Thalassodendron ciliatum* (right), *Thalassia hemprichii* (bottom left) and *Syringodium isoetifolium* (top left).

Mosses

Mosses (phylum Bryophyta) thrive in damp conditions, such as the upland forests of Mahé where tree branches may be covered in thick cushions of moss. They are generally small plants, without vascular tissue, and depend on water for sexual reproduction. However, some species survive even on the dry low coralline islands, for instance *Calymperes tenerum*, which can reproduce vegetatively, reducing its dependence on a sexual stage. There are at least 107 species in Seychelles, but only six species on Aldabra.

Lichens

Every lichen is an association of two organisms, a fungus and a single-celled alga. They grow on a variety of substrates, but in Seychelles are usually found attached to tree or Coconut stems, or rocks. Lichens are more resistant to desiccation than mosses, and many species can occur in coastal lowlands and coralline islands. At least 140 lichen species occur in the granitic Seychelles, and 45 on Aldabra. Most of these are encrusting or foliose species that grow in spreading patches close to the substrate. At higher altitudes in humid locations, branched lichens such as *Usnea* (pictured) may occur.

Seaweeds

Rocky shores in temperate regions are often dominated by dense growths of larger algae – plant-like organisms commonly called seaweeds. In Seychelles, seaweeds (collectively known as Gomon in Creole) are largely restricted to areas where they are rarely exposed to the air. Among the larger species is the brown seaweed *Sargassum cristaefolium* (pictured), pieces of which are commonly cast up on sandy beaches.

A Brief History

The Aldabra group and the low coralline islands of the Amirantes were known to Portuguese navigators in the early 16th century, and indeed Aldabra itself was probably known to earlier seafarers from the Arab world (its name perhaps originates in the Arabic *Al Khadra* – 'the green'). There is no definite record of the granitic islands until 1609 when a ship of the British East India Company inadvertently came across them.

Permanent settlement of Seychelles came much more recently. The granitic islands, with more abundant fresh water and better soils, were the first to be settled (by France) in 1770.

Settlement of the more remote coralline islands came in the 19th century, in order to exploit guano deposits and to replant with Coconuts, which thrived on coral islands. Coconut plantations became the mainstay of the economy after the abolition of slavery in 1835, and Coconuts were planted on most islands. In the later part of the 19th century (from 1888) even inhospitable Aldabra was settled in order to better exploit its natural resources – tortoises, turtles, seabirds, mangroves and fish.

In the 20th century, cinnamon became an important export crop in the granitic islands, with cinnamon oil distilled from the leaves, and the bark collected and dried. Later in the 20th century, the importance of coconuts and cinnamon declined as a result of pests and diseases, and competition from larger plantations elsewhere. A number of previously settled islands were all but abandoned. More recently, tourism has provided the incentive to re-settle many islands with the establishment of island resorts. Today, the economy of the country is dominated by the export of processed tuna and by the tourist trade, although small amounts of cinnamon are still collected in the hills of Mahé.

Scientific studies of Seychelles' flora and fauna lagged behind settlement and exploitation; by 1840, only two of the more than 80 endemic plants of the granitic islands had been described, and the endemic birds of the islands were only named in the second half of the 19th century. One of the characteristic trees of the mountain forest, the kapisen *Northea hornei*, was not known to science until 1883 when specimens were collected by the visiting botanical artist Marianne North. Several species of plant were only discovered in the last quarter of the 20th century. In fact, the endemic tree *Pisonia sechellarum*, of which only a few hundred trees survive in Silhouette's mountain forest, was first described as late as 1986. While there may be no more bird and few new plant species to be described, groups of smaller and less charismatic organisms such as fungi, insects and other invertebrates still contain many as-yet unknown species.

Climate and Tides

The climate of Seychelles is tropical and oceanic. There are two main seasons: between May and September, the South-east trade winds dominate the climate. From November to March, the North-west monsoon dominates. The South-east season is a period of low rainfall and strong winds (averaging 11 knots/21kmph) resulting in rough sea conditions. In contrast, the North-west is the rainy season, with peak rainfall in December–February (*see* graph). Winds are less strong and calms are frequent, so sea conditions are also generally calmer. The changeover periods of April and October are generally dry, with low variable winds and (usually) relatively calm seas.

The air temperature is equable throughout the year, the mean annual figure being approximately 26.8°C and with a mean daily range of +/-3.2°C. At higher altitudes on the large granitic islands temperatures are lower.

Rainfall varies through the country. The area of the Aldabra Atolls is the driest, with a mean annual total of rainfall around 1,200mm, although this does vary greatly from year to year. Rainfall is higher and more reliable on the granitic islands. At sea level on Mahé, the average total annual rainfall is 2,500mm, increasing at higher altitudes to 5,000mm. The highest peaks of Mahé and Silhouette may be wreathed in cloud at any time of year. Even at sea level, the air always remains humid, with relative humidity around 80 per cent all year.

Seychelles is well to the north of the normal path of cyclones in the Indian Ocean, although the passing of cyclones over the Mascarenes or Madagascar can sometimes cause stormy weather here.

The tidal range in Seychelles is relatively small; the maximum range at the granitic islands is 1.8m, and the range is less than 1m in neap tide periods. At Aldabra, the range is much greater (over 3m), causing the lagoon to empty partially at low tide. In comparison, the spring tidal range along the east coast of Africa is 2-5m.

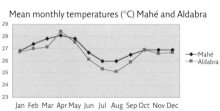

Mean monthly temperatures (°C) Mahé and Aldabra

Mean monthly rainfall (mm) Mahé and Aldabra

Conservation

Seychelles is one of the most recently settled oceanic island groups and, although the environment of the islands has been much altered since they were discovered by humans, they have escaped some of the worst environmental degradation that has occurred on many other Indian Ocean islands. Seychelles has fewer introduced animal species than Mauritius, for example, although it was once administered from that island. It has also suffered fewer extinctions; the hilly interior of the larger islands provides refuge for endemic plants, and the few smaller islands that have remained free of introduced predators support populations of endemic animals.

However, there have been extinctions, and fears for the future survival of charismatic and useful species, such as the Coco de Mer, Aldabra Giant Tortoise, turtles and seabirds, lead to the early introduction of legislation to manage exploitation of these species. In 1874, a group of eminent scientists including Charles Darwin petitioned to safeguard the giant tortoises of Aldabra, which were being harvested by the lessee of the atoll. In the 20th century, a range of other species and areas received protection.

The first protected areas were declared in 1966, when some of the smaller islands and the Vallée de Mai were designated as nature reserves. Seychelles now has three different types of protected area aimed at biodiversity conservation:

National Parks Two have been declared: Morne Seychellois National Park, Mahé; Praslin National Park, which includes the Vallée de Mai.

Marine Protected Areas Six marine national parks have been declared, and waters around the island special reserves (*see* below) are also protected: Silhouette; Curieuse Island (the land area of which is also protected); Sainte Anne Marine Park, Baie Ternay and Port Launay off Mahé; Île Cocos off Félicité/La Digue.

Special Reserves Four special reserves exist, within which all non-conservation activities are very strictly regulated: Aride Island; Cousin Island; Vev Reserve, La Digue; Aldabra.

All these protected areas can be visited, and in many cases entrance fees (or landing fees, for the island reserves) are charged, which go toward the maintenance of the sites. Entry to the Vev Reserve on La Digue, and both National Parks (with the exception of the Vallée de Mai) is free.

In addition to the designated sites named above, a number of privately-owned islands have policies in place to protect or enhance their biodiversity.

Examples include Bird Island, Cousine, Denis, Frégate and North Island. All these islands have taken important steps to restoring biodiversity value, for example through expensive operations to eradicate rats and other introduced predators. All of these islands have hotels or resorts.

Seychelles has two World Heritage Sites: the Vallée de Mai and Aldabra. These are among the 177 natural areas around the world recognised by UNESCO as being of outstanding universal value from the point of view of science, conservation or natural beauty. Both are managed by Seychelles Island Foundation (SIF). The Vallée de Mai is a popular day out and fees from visitors help support the management of remote Aldabra.

Non-Governmental Organisations (NGOs) have been a relatively recent development in Seychelles. The international organisations BirdLife International and the Wildlife Trusts (then known as ICBP and RSNC, respectively) have been managing sites in Seychelles since the late 1960s, but local organisations did not form until the 1980s. Now, there are at least seven organisations with different interests including: Nature Seychelles (NS; manages Cousin Island; www.natureseychelles.org); Seychelles Island Foundation (www.sif.sc); Island Conservation Society (ICS; manages Aride Island; www.arideisland.net); Nature Preservation Trust of Seychelles (NPTS; based on Silhouette; http://members.aol.com/jstgerlach); Marine Conservation Society of Seychelles (MCSS; www.mcss.sc); Wildlife Clubs of Seychelles (WCS) and the Plant Conservation Action group (PCA).

Today, cooperative programmes involving island owners, government and NGOs have been established to protect some of the most endangered species such as the Seychelles Magpie-robin, Seychelles Paradise Flycatcher and Seychelles White-eye. It now seems unlikely that any of the endemic birds will become extinct in the near future.

Unfortunately, research and conservation of animals other than birds, tortoises and turtles is still poorly developed. The threats that could lead to the extinction of endangered endemics still include habitat loss and direct exploitation (poaching), but both of these are perhaps less important than they have been at various times in the history of Seychelles. Development is a disproportionate threat to certain habitats, especially lowland marshes; many upland areas and small islands fall within protected areas. Poaching is a definite threat to certain species (such as turtles) and populations (breeding seabirds on unprotected islands). But perhaps the most important threats to wildlife are introduced species such as rats and cats, and a range of alien plants and invertebrates.

Notes for the Visitor

There are many general visitor guides to Seychelles and this section is not intended to be comprehensive, but is intended to offer a few useful hints for potential visitors.

The Republic of Seychelles covers a vast area, most of which is ocean. The only international airport, and main point of entry, is on Mahé. Entry formalities can only be completed at Mahé. Visitors from the EU and USA do not require visas for a stay of one month or less. Mahé is the largest of the granitic islands and has a range of tourist accommodation. From Mahé, Air Seychelles operates regular internal flights to the second island, Praslin, as well as to airstrips on smaller islands including Bird, Denis, Alphonse and Desroches. Praslin can also be reached by fast ferry from Port Victoria's Inter-island Quay, and La Digue by ferry from Praslin or by slow schooner from Mahé. Many islands have tourist developments, and more are being developed all the time, but generally these are exclusive, and expensive to stay at. Some resort islands, such as Frégate, Cousine and North, have programmes to protect and enhance their biodiversity. Cheaper accommodation is available on Mahé, Praslin and La Digue.

For the tourist visiting the granitic islands, a minimum itinerary would be a few days on Mahé (for hill walking and to see a range of endemic species), Praslin (to visit the Vallée de Mai and as a base for day trips to the seabird islands of Aride or Cousin, and Curieuse for its wild tortoises) and La Digue (for the Seychelles Paradise Flycatcher and beaches). In particular, a short trip to Bird Island (at least two nights) is recommended during the Sooty Tern breeding season from March to October. For keen birdwatchers who want to see all the endemic birds of the granitic islands, this itinerary should ensure sightings of all endemics except possibly the Seychelles White-eye and Scops Owl; for these birds, a local guide is probably necessary and can be arranged through travel agents or tourist information.

Generally, the coralline islands are less accessible than the granitics. Closest to Mahé, Bird and Denis islands sit on the edge of the Seychelles Bank and each has a single hotel. There are hotels on some of the Amirantes including Alphonse and Desroches, with others under construction. Many of the Amirantes, and the Aldabra group, are only accessible by sea. Aldabra can be visited on board a cruise ship or private vessel.

The best time to visit Seychelles depends upon your interest. Most seabirds will be breeding in the dry South-East season, from around April to September, although a few species, particularly the Fairy Tern and White-tailed Tropicbird, breed year-round. However, sea conditions can be rough at this time, reducing visibility when snorkelling and making some islands inaccessible. Rainfall is heaviest in December and January, during the North-West monsoon, but the sea is usually calmer in this season. Seasonal migrant birds and vagrants are seen in the period October to March or April.

Natural Dangers

Compared with many other tropical countries, there are relatively few dangerous or unpleasant creatures in Seychelles. On land, there are no poisonous snakes. Biting and stinging invertebrates are few; the most likely to sting is the Yellow Wasp, which makes a hanging paper nest in vegetation (particularly under the leaves of young Coconut Palms), and will attack when it thinks it is threatened. Giant Millipedes do not bite but secrete an irritant substance, and Giant Centipedes have a potentially very painful bite but will only bite when provoked. They are common on some of the coral islands and are mainly active at night, so you should wear shoes at night to avoid stepping on them with bare feet. Scorpions will also sting when provoked. Mosquitoes are an unpleasant nuisance. Seychelles is free of malaria although there are occasional outbreaks of dengue fever, which can be very unpleasant. Mosquito repellents are recommended especially if visiting woodland areas and nature reserves. On beaches, sand flies are a nuisance and are unaffected by many mosquito repellents. Antihistamine cream should ease the itchy bites.

There are greater dangers at sea. Large sharks are rather rare close to the granitic islands but more common in less disturbed areas such as Aldabra. Shark attacks are extremely rare in Seychelles. In some places, such as the lagoons of less disturbed atolls, Stingrays are common. All have a barbed spine on or at the base of the tail and can give a painful or potentially dangerous sting. Other potentially dangerous fish include the Stonefish, Lionfish, and the Turkeyfish. The Stonefish is uncommon but is potentially fatal; the animal is highly camouflaged and the dorsal spines can penetrate bare skin and inject venom. Always wear something on your feet when reef walking. If stung, there is a specific antivenom but this may not always be available – alternative treatments include immersing the wound in hot water as soon as possible to denature the venom. Other fish with venomous spines (including Lionfish, Rabbitfish, marine catfish and surgeon fish) are conspicuous and will tend to avoid humans. Needlefish and Garfish will occasionally leap from the water and can pierce the skin with their sharp beaks. Cone shells have poison darts, used to kill prey, and some can kill a human. Live cone shells should not be handled. Jellyfish and Portuguese Man-o'-war have stings that may be severe, but are rarely a problem. Much more common is a mild irritating itch after swimming, caused by small hydroids or medusae. Corals and sea urchins are also common marine dangers. Long-spined urchins are common on rocky substrate in shallow places, and when brushed against, spines tend to lodge in the skin and are painful and difficult to remove. Thin spines that cannot be removed will disappear with time. Corals can cause cuts and burns; coral scratches should be treated with antiseptic and left to dry.

Cuts and infected bites from many sources can become rapidly and severely inflamed and may need antibiotic treatment, to which they normally respond well.

Many of the dangers in Seychelles are physical. You should be aware of the power of the sun (especially when swimming) and use sunscreen. Dehydration should be avoided. Some beaches have dangerous currents; these beaches are generally marked as such on tourist maps. On land, granite slopes can become very slippery when wet.

Walks and Highlights

Mahé

Mahé is the most developed of the islands, and most beaches and coastal areas are easily accessible by car. There are a number of well-marked trails in the hills, most of which are relatively short and easy if you are reasonably fit. Some of the best are described below, and guides to these and other trails are available at tourist information in Victoria. The highest point of Morne Seychellois (905m) can be reached on foot but the path is difficult and should not be attempted without someone who has been before. Similarly, the beautiful moss forests of Congo Rouge are best accessed with a guide.

1. TROIS FRÈRES TRAIL This trail starts from the Sans Souci forest station on the Sans Souci road. It begins in a forested area, made up of Cinnamon *Cinnamomum verum*, Kalis Dipap *Tabebuia pallida*, mahogany *Swietenia* sp. and introduced palms. At higher altitudes there are scrubby areas of Cocoplum *Chrysobalanus icaco* and Lemon Grass *Cymbopogon* sp. The path ends at an open area of glacis, with a range of endemic plants including *Pandanus multispicatus*, *Memecylon eleagni* and *Nepenthes pervillei*. The visitor shelter at about 460m above sea level marks the end of the path; it is possible to continue up to the concrete cross on the mountain above although the path is rather eroded. Birds that may be seen include the Seychelles Sunbird and Bulbul.

2. COPOLIA TRAIL Copolia is a prominent hill jutting towards the east coast of Mahé. The well-marked trail is a little over 1km long and starts from the Sans Souci road, just above India House and before the nursery. The walk can be accessed by SPTC bus (Victoria to Port Launay). It will take between half an hour and an hour to reach the top. Near the beginning of the path, there is a large Koko Maron plant *Curculigo sechellensis*. The Copolia walk begins in mixed forest, passing through an area with Cinnamon, Kalis Dipap, Rubber and planted Takamaka trees. Higher up the path, endemic palms are common including *Nephrosperma vanhoutteanum*, *Phoenicophorium borsigianum* and *Vershaffeltia splendida*. Other endemic plants include the trees and shrubs *Dillenia ferruginea*, *Mimusops sechellarum*, *Memecylon eleagni* and *Pandanus sechellarum*. Understorey herbs include the endemic sedge *Mapania floribunda* and Pti Koko Maron *Hypoxidia rhizophylla*. At the top of the trail, there is an open area of glacis with views towards Praslin. Vegetation here is dominated by the endemic dwarf pandanus *Pandanus multispicatus*, the sedge *Lophoschoenus hornei* and *Nepenthes pervillei*. The highest point here is 497m above sea level.

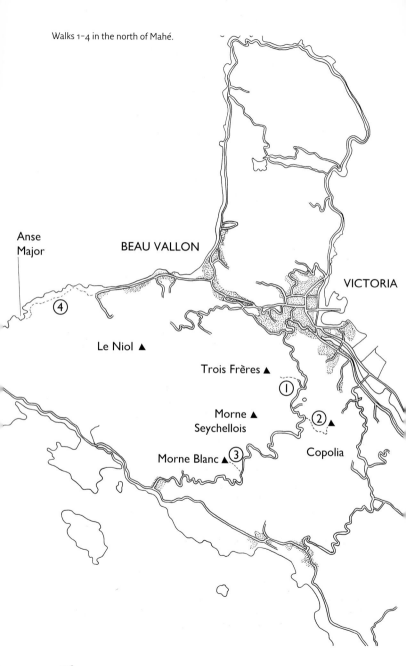

Walks 1–4 in the north of Mahé.

Anse
Major

BEAU VALLON

VICTORIA

Le Niol ▲

Trois Frères ▲

④

①

Morne ▲
Seychellois

②▲

Copolia

Morne Blanc ▲③

3. MORNE BLANC Morne Blanc is another short, steep trail leading to a lookout point. In this case, the view is of the west coast of Mahé. The trail starts from the Sans Souci road just before the Tea Tavern (travelling from Victoria). The trail starts among tea plantations and lemon grass. The initial upward stretch of the path is open and grassy, with *Cynorkis* orchids in the grass, Koko Maron *Curculigo sechellensis*, Bracken Fern *Dicranopteris linearis* and Bwa Rouz *Dillenia ferruginea* trees. Further up, the forest of Cinnamon *Cinnamomum verum* closes. The higher forest area is dominated by some huge old Sandragon *Pterocarpus indicus* trees, loaded with epiphytic ferns. Among the larger terrestrial ferns found here are the Seychelles Tree Fern *Cyathea sechellarum* and Baton Monsennyer *Angiopteris evecta*. This is a good area for stick insects and endemic sooglossid frogs. The path flattens out here in an area of short, moist forest rich in endemic species and epiphytic plants. The trees include Kapisen *Northea hornei* as well as introduced Cinnamon and Chinese Guava *Psidium cattleianum*. Other plants include orchids such as *Malaxis seychellarum*. Animals to be seen on the track include the Seychelles Bulbul, Sunbird, Tenrec and the Seychelles Wolf Snake. The highest point here is 667m. From the viewpoint, there is a very good view of the west coast of Mahé.

4. ANSE MAJOR TRAIL Anse Major is a small attractive beach only accessible on foot. The path begins at Belombre, reached by bus (get off at La Scala restaurant, where the bus turns around). Follow the road through an area of gardens and trees (keep right) until the quality of the road deteriorates and the habitat alternates between Cocoplum scrub and Cinnamon woodland. Species to be seen here include *Canthium bibracteatum*, Cashew *Anacardium occidentale*, Vanilla *Vanilla planifolia*, Pineapple *Ananas comosus* and several endemic palms. For much of the coastal walk, the path passes over open rocky areas with a range of introduced and endemic vegetation including Cocoplum, Lantana *Lantana camara*, *Furcraea foetida*, Casuarina *Casuarina equisetifolia*, palms, Bwa Kalou *Memecylon eleagni* and endemic Vanilla *Vanilla phalaenopsis*. Common bird species include the Indian Mynah and Seychelles Bulbul.

Islands of the Ste Anne Marine Park

The islands of the Ste Anne Marine Park are accessible from Mahé, with day trips to Round, Moyenne and Cerf. The vegetation of the smaller islands tends to be dominated by introduced species (Cerf Island, with a number of endemics on the hill, is the exception). Marine life in the park has been badly affected by El Niño, as well as by dredging to complete the East Coast reclamation project and other development.

PRASLIN This is the second largest of the granitic islands. The greatest conservation interest is undoubtedly the Coco de Mer forests of Vallée de Mai and Fond Ferdinand. Vallée de Mai is managed by the Seychelles Island Foundation. It is open daily and can be reached by bus (from Grande Anse to Baie Ste Anne) or taxi. Here, the forest includes most of Seychelles' endemic palms and pandanus, and a range of other interesting endemics, although it is the Coco de Mer that steals the show.

ISLANDS OFF PRASLIN Aride and Cousin are similar reserve islands off Praslin. Aride is larger, with a greater variety of nesting seabirds while Cousin has extensive *Pisonia* forests and endemic land birds. Cousin is open all year round and is relatively close to Praslin. Aride is further out and is sometimes inaccessible. Both can be reached as part of a package day-trip offered by tourism operators, or independently by hiring a boat.

Curieuse is a larger island and was formerly a leper colony. It is now a marine park. Terrestrial ecosystems are interesting, with Coco de Mer palms growing in dry scrub on the hills and with extensive mangrove. There is a large breeding herd of wild, free-roaming Aldabra Giant Tortoises. Curieuse can be reached by small boat from Côte d'Or on Praslin.

All these islands have a landing charge.

LA DIGUE La Digue has a small nature reserve, the Vev Reserve, designated to protect the endemic Seychelles Paradise Flycatcher, which is now only found here. However, flycatchers are widespread in the plateau forests of La Digue. The marshy plateau is also a good place to observe endemic terrapins, tree frogs and the Yellow Bittern. The hilly part of La Digue also has a range of interesting species including endemic palms.

ISLANDS OFF LA DIGUE Île Cocos is a marine park and offers good snorkelling. The tiny island itself is covered with native figs and Coconuts.

Snorkelling is also possible off Grande Soeur but the island itself is rather degraded, with abundant Cinnamon and Cocoplum.

Glossary

ADAPTIVE RADIATION The evolution of a range of species from a single common ancestor. An obvious feature of fauna and flora on many island groups.

ADVENTITIOUS ROOTS (of plants) Roots arising directly from the aerial part of the stem. May occur, for example, on the stems of trees in humid moss forest.

ANAL FINS (of fish) The fin on the lower side of a fish, immediately behind the anus.

ANOXIC Lacking oxygen, e.g. waterlogged sediments of mangrove forest.

ARIL (of plants) A fleshy covering of a seed, sometimes brightly coloured to attract dispersal agents such as birds.

BRACT (of plants) A modified leaf at the base of the flower-stalk. Sometimes brightly coloured, resembling petals and having the same ecological function; e.g. in *Bougainvillea*, *Poinsettia*.

BUTTRESS (of plants) A flange-like supporting structure at the base of a tree trunk.

BYSSUS (of bivalves) A tuft of tough silky filaments by which some molluscs adhere to rocks.

CALYX (of plants) The sepals; tough, usually green segments that often surround the petals, protecting the flower bud. Sometimes, calyx segments may resemble petals.

CARAPACE (of tortoises, terrapins and turtles) The upper 'shell' of a tortoise, composed of bony plates fused to the backbone, covered with horny scutes.

CAUDAL FIN (of fish) The tail fin of a fish.

COLUMELLA (of molluscs) The glossy inner lip of a gastropod mollusc shell.

COMPOUND LEAVES (of plants) A leaf form; where each leaf is composed of more than one leaflet.

COROLLA (of plants) The petals of a flower.

CREPUSCULAR Active at twilight.

CUPULE (of plants) A cup-like structure enclosing the seed of some plants.

DIMORPHISM A species which has two different forms or varieties is said to be dimorphic. Many animals exhibit sexual dimorphism, with the male and female having different colour, pattern or size.

DIURNAL Active by day.

DORSAL FIN (of fish) The fins along the back of fish and some marine mammals.

ENDEMIC A species found in one place (e.g. the granitic Seychelles) and nowhere else on earth, is said to be *endemic* to that place.

Epiphyte/Epiphytic (of plants) A plant that has no root connections with the soil but grows on another plant or tree, using it for support. Not a parasite – it gains no nutrition from the support plant.

Established Introduced species are said to have become established in a location when breeding means that recruitment to the population (births) exceeds natural loss (deaths), i.e. when the population begins to grow.

Genus (plural: genera) A taxonomic division above species; a group of closely related species with a shared evolutionary history.

Introduced A breeding population of a species outside that species' natural range, having arrived there through human transport, is said to be *introduced*.

Liane/Liana (of plants) A long-stemmed climbing plant or vine. Usually rooted in the ground but its stems are supported by other plant hosts. Derives no nutrients from the host.

Migrant Migration is a regular (usually seasonal or annual) movement of individuals along a predictable route. In Seychelles, many wading birds are migrants, occurring here during the northern winter and returning to the far north to breed.

Morph A recurring distinct physical variant within a species, e.g. one of two or more colour variants. Different morphs of the same species can occur in the same population.

Native Within their natural range (i.e. before human-mediated introductions) species are said to be *native*.

Neap tide The period of minimum tidal range (opposite of spring tide).

Nocturnal Active by night.

Old World In biogeography, a term referring to the continents of Africa, Europe and Asia. The New World is the Americas.

Operculum (of molluscs) A plate covering the aperture of a gastropod mollusc's shell.

Ovate (of plants) A leaf shape; almost round, but with a pointed tip.

Parthenogenesis Or 'virgin birth'; a means of producing eggs or young without sexual reproduction. Occurs most frequently in insects, but the Brahminy Blind Snake is a rare example of a reptile that reproduces only by parthenogenesis.

Pectoral fin (of fish) Fins projecting from the side of a fish directly behind the gills.

Pelagic (of marine creatures) Occurring in the open sea.

Peltate (of plants) A leaf shape; with the leaf stalk joining the leaf in the middle (not at the margin), similar to water-lily leaves.

Pelvic fin (of fish) The paired fins below and behind the gills.

Perianth (of plants) The collective name for the calyx and corolla, used especially where the two are similar.

PERICARP (of plants) The wall of a fruit, derived from the ovary wall.

PINNATE (of plants) A leaf shape; with leaflets either side of a central stem.

PLASTRON (of tortoises, turtles or terrapins) The underside of a tortoise shell, made up of bone covered by horny plates (scutes). Cf. *Carapace*.

PNEUMATOPHORE (of plants) A mangrove's 'breathing root', projecting above anoxic sediments and allowing oxygen for respiration to reach the rest of the root system.

PSEUDOBULB (of plants) The storage organ of certain orchid species (e.g. Pigeon Orchid); a swollen, bulb-like section of stem at the base of the leafy stem and arising from the rhizome.

RESIDENT (of birds) Birds that occur in an area year-round without migrating, or undergoing only very localised seasonal movements.

RHIZOME (of plants) An underground storage organ of plants; a root-like modified stem, often swollen and usually horizontally creeping.

SPORANGIA (of ferns) Spore-producing tissues.

SPRING TIDE A period of maximum tidal range; very high high tide and very low low tide. Spring tides occur twice a month when the moon and sun (both gravitational influences on the tide) are in alignment.

STAMENS (of plants) The male reproductive parts of a flower, each usually divided into a pollen-bearing anther at the tip of a long filament.

STYLE (of plants) The long structure that supports the female part of a flower (the stigma) and may remain attached to the maturing fruit.

SYMBIOSIS Two species living together for their mutual benefit, e.g. a coral polyp and microscopic algal cells.

UMBILICUS (of molluscs) Aperture in the central pillar of a snail shell, visible from beneath.

VAGRANT (of birds) A species carried outside its natural range by freak weather conditions. Most vagrant birds in Seychelles occur in November to March, when migrating flocks passing along the coast of Africa are blown off course.

WHORL (of molluscs) A single coil of the shell of a gastropod mollusc.

Bibliography and Further Reading

A number of books exist on different elements of the flora and fauna of Seychelles, but unfortunately most are out of print. Key works are identified with an asterisk *.

Birds
Nature Seychelles (2004) *Discover Seychelles' Birds*. Nature Seychelles, Victoria.
Skerrett, A., Bullock, I. & Disley, T. (2001) *Birds of Seychelles*. Christopher Helm, London. *

Fish
Debelius, H. (1993) *Indian Ocean – Tropical Fish Guide*. Aquaprint Verlags, Neu Isenburg, Germany.
Lieske, E. & Myers, R. (1994) *Coral Reef Fishes: Caribbean, Indian Ocean and Pacific Ocean*. Collins Pocket Guide. HarperCollins, London. *
Polunin, N.V.C. & Williams, F.R.J. (1977) *Coral Reef Fish of Seychelles*. Seychelles Nature Handbook No. 8. Government Printer, Hong Kong.
Smith, J.L.B. & Smith, M.M. (1963) *Fishes of the Seychelles*. Rhodes University, Grahamstown.

Marine Invertebrates
Debelius, H. (1999) *Indian Ocean Reef Guide*. IKAN Unterwasser Archiv, Frankfurt.
Jarrett, A.G. (2000) *Marine Shells of the Seychelles*. Carole Green Publishing, Cambridge.
Richmond, M.D. (ed.) (1997) *A Guide to the Seashores of Eastern Africa and the Western Indian Ocean Islands*. SIDA/Dept. for Research Cooperation, SAREC. *
The last volume includes coverage of a wide range of other groups such as fish, birds, and plants.

Plants
Fosberg, F. & Renvoize, S. (1980) Flora of Aldabra and neighbouring islands. *Kew Bulletin Additional Series* Vol. 7, pp. 1–358. *
Friedmann, F. (1994) *Flore des Seychelles: Vol. 1 Dicotylédones*. Éditions de l'Orstom, Paris. *
Lötscher, W. & Beese, G. (1983) *Collins Photoguide to Tropical Plants*. HarperCollins Publishers, London.
Robertson, S.A. (1979) *Flowering Plants of Seychelles*. Royal Botanic Gardens, Kew.

Wise, R. (1998) *A Fragile Eden: Portraits of the Endemic Flowering Plants of the Granitic Seychelles*. Princeton University Press, Princeton, NJ.
Endemic plants are beautifully illustrated in the Rosemary Wise book. Introduced plants found throughout the tropics are well covered in the Collins guide. The other books are comprehensive guides to flora but all are out of print.

Terrestrial Invertebrates

Blackman, R.A.A. & Pinhey, E.C.G. (1967) Odonata of the Seychelles and other Indian Ocean island groups based primarily on the Bristol University Expedition of 1964-65. *Arnoldia (Rhodesia)* Vol. 3, pp. 1-38.
Gerlach, J. (1987) *The Land Snails of Seychelles. A Field Guide*. Privately published.
Gerlach, J. (1999) Snails of the genus *Pachnodus (Mollusca; Gastropoda; Enidae): Their Origins and Evolution. Journal of Biogeography* Vol. 24, pp. 251-255.
Legrand, H. (1966) Lépidoptères des Îles Seychelles et d'Aldabra. *Mémoires du Muséum National d'Histoire Naturelle*, Sér. A, Vol. 37, pp. 1-210, 16 plates.
There is a dearth of books on the invertebrates of Seychelles. Those looking for further information will need to study scientific papers, many of them dating from early in the 20th century; a few examples are given above.

General Ecology

Stoddart, D.R. (ed.) (1984) *Biogeography and Ecology of the Seychelles Islands*. Dr. W. Junk Publishers, The Hague.
The most authoritative volume on the subject, covering a wide area of interest: unfortunately out of print and hard to find.

Index

Acknowledgements

Any book of this nature is bound to involve creative input from a range of people and the authors would like to acknowledge and thank the many people in Seychelles and beyond who have assisted greatly in its production, while accepting complete responsibility for any errors in this volume.

In particular, we would like to thank Pat Matyot for his invaluable advice on everything from lizards to dragonflies, Nirmal Jivan Shah for advice and assistance with Creole names, Eva Schumacher and Christoph Kueffer for sharing their knowledge of Seychelles' botany, Dr Jeanne Mortimer for assistance with the text on turtles, Dr Justin Gerlach for information on geckoes, Dr Marie-Louise Cariou for information on *Drosophila sechellia*, and Professor Michael Saaristo for information on spiders. In Britain, we would like to thank all those who have contributed to the layout and text of the book, and especially Emily Pitcher at Collins, without whom this book would never have happened.

The authors' work in the Seychelles would have been impossible without the conservation organisation Nature Seychelles (or BirdLife Seychelles, as it was then called), and we would like to thank all the staff of that organisation. The list of those who have shared their field knowledge and otherwise given support is long and includes: Katy Beaver, Lindsay Chong-Seng, Rodney Fanchette, Clive Hambler, Steve Parr, Camille Hoareau, Rachel and Unels Bristol, and Terrence Vel – and many others. Several photographers have allowed us to reproduce their excellent pictures in this book; photographic credits are given below. Thanks to them all. We hope that this book in a small way helps to inspire interest in Seychelles wildlife and we would like to acknowledge all individuals and organisations committed to conservation of Seychelles and its natural beauty, and wish them well in their future endeavours.

Photographic Credits

All images © Dave Currie, except for the following: pp. 18b, 100 (2 down), 100b © Kelvin Aitken/marinethemes.com; 14lt © Laura Bambini; 166tl, 216tr © Katy Beaver; 22br, 30b, 46tr, 48t, 50bl, 52b, 54b, 54tl, 56br, 58ml, 62b, 62t, 66b, 72t, 80br, 86 (3 down), 142b, 166tr, 208br, 238tr © Michael Betts; 184b, 190t, 230tr © Rachel Bristol; 56tl© Unels Bristol; 42br, 44tl © Richard Brooks/FLPA; 16mr, 22tr, 22bl, 24t, 24br, 24m, 32m, 34bl, 34br, 38m, 190m © Alan Burger; 158b © Marie-Louise Cariou; 38t © Lindsay Chong-Seng; 42mr © Robert Canis/FLPA; 32b © David A Currie; 52tr © Bill Coster/NHPA; 30t © Nigel J. Denis/NHPA; 100t © Steve Drogin/marinethemes.com; 40mr © Guy Edwardes/-NHPA; 14tr, 86b © Nick Garbutt; 78b © Kalid Ghani/NHPA; 18m © Saul Gonor/-marinethemes.com; 76b, 84b, 128tr, 128 (3 down)l, 130 (2 down), 142ml, 142tl, 148b, 174tm, 174tr, 174mr, 174b, 176mr, 176t, 176ml, 178br, 178bl, 180b, 182tl, 182tr, 184ml, 186b, 186t, 188tl, 188tr, 188ml, 188mr, 188m, 192bl, 192br, 194t, 194mr, 194b, 196mr, 196ml, 198br, 198bl, 200t, 200t, 200m, 200b, 202l, 202r, 204m, 204br, 212br, 216mr, 216tl, 216tm, 220t, 220l, 220r, 224tl, 224tr, 226tl, 226tr, 228ml, 230tl, 232t, 232ml, 234b, 240tl, 240tr, 240mr, 240ml, 240b, 242tr, 242ml, 242mr, 242b, 242tl, 244m, 246t, 246mr, 248tl, 248b © Mike Hill; 56tl © John Holmes/FLPA; 36b, 64bl © David Hoskings/FLPA; 96t, 146b, 214t © Kirsi Laitio; 82m © Chris Mattison/FLPA; 220b, 222b, 238tl © Kieran Millar; 44tr, 44br © Flip de Nooyer/Foto Natura/FLPA; 26b © Pete Oxford/Nature PL; 94 © Jeff Rotman/Nature PL; 82b, 90t, 90m, 90bl, 90br, 168bl, 168br, 174ml, 182bl, 184ml, 192tr, 210ml, 214bl, 224ml,224mr,238bl, 244tr, 246ml © Eva Schumacher; 64br © Jurgen and Christine Sohns/FLPA; 36ml © Lynn M. Stone/Nature PL; 52tl © James Warwick/NHPA; 18t © Stephen Wong/marinethemes.com; 14bl, 164m © Gary Woodburn; 46b © Steve Young/FLPA.

tl = top left; tr= top right; m = middle; br = bottom right; bl = bottom left